Illuminated Manuscripts and their Makers

Dilexi quoniam
exaudiet dñs vo
cem orõnis mee.

ILLUMINATED MANUSCRIPTS AND THEIR MAKERS

ROWAN WATSON

An account based on the collection of the Victoria and Albert Museum

V&A Publications

Reproductions rarely prepare the reader for the impact of meeting any original illuminated manuscript. Rather than attempt to reproduce the details, pages and openings of manuscripts illustrated in this book in the same size as the originals, it was decided to let the design of a modern book govern the scale of reproduction. This has the advantage of magnifying, in some cases, the elements to which the text draws attention, and in others of allowing large illuminations to be included within the format of this book.

First published by V&A Publications, 2003
V&A Publications
160 Brompton Road
London SW3 1HW

Rowan Watson asserts his moral right to be identified as the author of this book

Designed by Bernard Higton
Photography by Sara Hodges and Philip Barnard of the V&A Photographic Studio

ISBN 1 85177 386 X

A catalogue record for this book is available from the British Library

Every effort has been made to seek permission to reproduce those images whose copyright does not reside with the V&A, and we are grateful to the individuals and institutions who have assisted in this task. Any omissions are entirely unintentional, and the details should be addressed to V&A Publications.

Printed in Hong Kong

Front cover: St Anthony, from the Margaret de Foix Hours. France, *c.*1471–76. MSL/1910/2385 (Salting 1222), f.209.

Back cover: Burial scene and Requiem Mass from a Book of Hours. France, *c.*1400–10. MSL/1902/1646 (Reid 4), f.179v-180.
Petrarch's *Rime*, second part, poems on the death of Laura. Italy (Padua), *c.*1463–64. MSL/1947/101, f.106.
Initial *S* for Psalm 68, from a Psalter. Germany, mid-13th century. MSL/1870/7789, f.96.
Ornament from a choirbook. Italy, late 15th century. PDP,4918.7.
Border ornament from the Bentivoglio Hours. Italy, *c.*1500. MSL/1902/1707 (Reid 64), f.33.

Frontispiece: Funeral scene, from a Book of Hours. France, *c.*1430–40. MSL/1894/181, f.48.

V&A Publications
160 Brompton Road
London SW3 1HW
www.vam.ac.uk

CONTENTS

PREFACE

ILLUMINATED MANUSCRIPTS are commonly counted as among the finest works of art produced in the Middle Ages. As a category of object, perception of them is perhaps unduly governed by a number of outstanding works – the seventh-century Book of Kells, The Très Riches Heures of the Duc de Berry, left incomplete in 1416, or the Bedford Missal, a Book of Hours made in Paris in the 1420s – which are certainly not typical of what survives in libraries and collections around Europe and North America today. These productions are described in many accounts of medieval art in Europe. The study of other, less exalted manuscripts, from the routine to the outstanding, allows us to approach illuminated manuscripts from a variety of perspectives, and to examine how they were made and used, and the changing ways in which they were appreciated in the centuries after the invention of printing.

The word 'illumination' has had a varied history. It was once used to describe the sweat-shop activity of colouring maps and prints. It was also used in a pejorative sense: a reviewer in *Punch* damned the Pre-Raphaelite paintings in the 1849 Royal Academy exhibition as having a 'quaintness that do smack of . . . illuminated Missals'. But in the nineteenth century the term 'illumination' became accepted to describe rich ornament in colours and gold added to books. In medieval times, the term could be used for any ornament used to make a text legible. Illumination might consist of simple blue and red initials, penwork flourishing or rich borders, decorative initials and miniatures; or it might include pictures that needed to be considered at the same time as the text, as in Books of Hours. When medieval books were not the informal jottings of a student or the working book of a lawyer, they were usually polychromatic, and thus, for us, illuminated.

The kind of book that we use today dates from the third and fourth centuries, when the scroll was abandoned in favour of the codex. Manuscript books were produced throughout the Middle Ages, mostly in monastic or court environments up to the twelfth century and from the thirteenth century by a commercial book trade. They were made for kings, clerics, doctors, lawyers, merchants and bureaucrats. Where have surviving manuscripts been until today, how do they come down to us? This matter of transmission, of provenance, is a significant part of looking at medieval books, since it enables us to see how different generations valued them to suit the intellectual agendas of their day as well as to explain their present locations.

Illuminated manuscripts can be found today in a variety of places. A few are in the buildings for which they were intended, from cathedral churches and colleges to stately homes and municipal archives. Others are in private hands, collected for their textual or artistic interest (mainly by connoisseurs in the eighteenth century, before a huge market developed in the nineteenth as part of what we call the Gothic Revival). The bulk today are in libraries and museums, and thus available for exhibitions and study. The great scholarly effort that began in the nineteenth century means that most of the larger collections have some kind of catalogue to describe their contents. For England, the volumes of Neil Ker's *Medieval Manuscripts in British Libraries* (1969 onwards) provide a starting point in the search for books written before 1500 by describing the contents of known repositories. While the published literature on illuminated manuscripts grows year by year, the Internet is also becoming an important source of access – some libraries use their websites to give a complete account of their holdings (e.g. the Royal Library in The Hague: www.kb.nl).

The aim of this book is to give an account of illuminated manuscripts held in the Victoria and Albert Museum, to say something of how they were made, and to suggest ways in which they can be studied. It also aims to explain why a museum of the decorative arts, founded to carry forward the ideals of the Great Exhibition of 1851 – in other words the effort to marry art and industry – saw fit to include such things in its collections. Illuminated manuscripts are extraordinarily attractive visually. They appear regularly in exhibitions, and have been reproduced in books from even before the 1840s, when new colour-printing technologies made this economically feasible. Even in our environment that is saturated by colour images, the technical achievement of medieval illuminators still arrests the eye. As in any field of research, there is debate about how to study them; this book outlines some of the differences in method in approaching illuminated manuscripts, on the grounds that such disagreement is both productive and enjoyable.

Of the many excellent works on illuminated manuscripts available today, those by Christopher de Hamel and Jonathan Alexander have provided magnificent guides to the subject as a whole. This book discusses illumination through a collection made specifically as an educational resource in the nineteenth century, a resource to which were added, from the 1890s, outstanding examples of the illuminator's art as the Museum itself sought to shrug off its association with 'industrial art' in order to redefine itself as an art museum. After a discussion of the medieval book trade, various elements that make up the illuminated page are examined. Investigation of mass-produced medieval books is followed by a 'Procession of Manuscripts', in which the intention is to set each work in context and, by providing some bibliographical references (in English where possible), to allow projects to be set up to study particular works. The method is impressionistic and the selection of examples idiosyncratic, but it is hoped that the plates and information presented will forward the purposes for which the collection was brought together, namely the use of original sources to examine questions of history and design.

I

The Medieval Book Trade

Terms such as 'book trade' and 'book industry' can appear surprising when applied to medieval manuscripts. They draw parallels between medieval conditions and the publishing environment of modern times, suggesting regular production, a settled means of marketing, and a commercial background similar to other manufactures of the period. Nevertheless, they are useful terms for discussing medieval book production. As well as centres where the term 'industry' seems appropriate, there was also a 'bespoke' production in which book-makers might join a noble household as retainers; dispersed scribes or illuminators filling specific orders might be better characterized as a cottage industry. This chapter suggests that there was a plurality of environments in which books were produced. Awareness of the circumstances of production will make it possible to enjoy both the complete manuscripts and the fragments of works reproduced in this book equally as historical documents and as objects of delight.

Before about 1200 monasteries and other ecclesiastical institutions were major centres of study and learning, just as they were economic and government centres. Some had regular provision for the making of books, a scriptorium which we can identify by the codicological features (i.e. physical aspects such as the writing support – parchment or paper – and details of ruling, sewing, binding, etc.), script and decoration of the books produced there. It is clear that in the eleventh and twelfth centuries there were lay scribes and illuminators who travelled from monastery to monastery. The books' appearance was dictated by their employers. There were standards that had to be followed, so that a cleric from Germany would have little difficulty in using a book made in France or England.

From about 1200 books began to be produced by lay people who were established in particular cities and who earned their living by making books. They had taxes to pay and civic responsibilities. Churchmen, too, continued to produce books, and many orders made their own. Carthusian monks, who lived almost as hermits in separate cells around a church under the authority of an abbot, had the duty of copying books. They were particularly successful in the fourteenth century, when the bureaucracy of church and secular government prompted a fundamentalist drive to seek isolation and union with God through meditation and personal devotional exercises. Gerard Groote (1340–84) aimed to improve the faith and morality of the laity through the promotion of ascetic exercises and personal devotions, as well as to revive monastic life by more rigorous concentration on spiritual matters. He set up many communities throughout the Low Countries for both lay people and clerics as part of the *Devotio moderna* movement. The Brethren of the Common Life set up communities in Deventer and Zwolle, and book production was among the activities by which they earned their living. This was an area where, uncharacteristically for Europe, monastic production in the fifteenth century was a significant element in the book trade. The statutes of some monastic houses where books were made have rules for the management of contracts with clients.

Some monasteries in other regions made illumination a speciality. From the last quarter of the fourteenth century, Santa Maria degli Angeli in Florence, a house of the

Camaldolese order, was the base of Don Silvestro dei Gherarducci and then of Lorenzo Monaco, who produced work for both their own house and for other patrons. The Camaldolese monk Don Silvestro worked mainly for other church institutions and for lay patrons. This was a meeting point for scholars and collectors, yet it probably also relied on a secular book trade for materials (parchment, pigments) and for other skills such as the preparation of sheets, writing and binding. Leonardo Bruni wrote in 1416 to a friend to regret that he could not find a suitable text of Priscian, the sixth-century Latin grammarian, even after looking in every bookshop in Florence ('*omnes tabernas librarias*'). By the early 1430s, the stationers' shops (*cartolai*) near the Badia and the Bargello were a centre of book production in Florence – in 1441 there were twelve *cartolai* here paying rent to the Badia alone. A scholar such as Bartolomeo Fazio wrote from Naples in 1448 to complain of the relative poverty of bookshops there compared to the Tuscan capital. The book trade was to become increasingly secular. In Germany, the chronicle of the Augsburg monastery of Saints Ulrich and Afra has a lot to say about books produced there, but it makes clear that there was dependence on the book trade for some elements: a Psalter written in the abbey *c.*1480–2 was sent into the city to the lay illuminators Georg Beck and his son.

From the church's point of view, there were dangers in total reliance on the secular book trade. In around 1265, the controversial philosopher and scientist Roger Bacon lamented his predicament. He wanted to send a copy of a treatise to Pope Clement IV; there were abundant scribes in his order (he was a Franciscan), but none could be relied on to produce writing to a suitable quality ('*litterae bonae*'). If he sent his script to a bookshop in Paris, the fair copy made would be inaccurate and, given the fraudulent nature of the Paris book trade, he would lose control of the text itself. This commercial environment was difficult for the ecclesiastical authorities to control. By 1274 Gilbert de Tournai could complain that texts of the Bible *in French* were publicly available at Parisian booksellers (*libraires*) – these might be tolerated for the king and his court, but there were dangerous implications if everybody could have them. This was a perennial problem: Petrarch in 1363 lamented that a copy of his epic *Africa* got into the hands of copyists before final correction, and Boccaccio was similarly concerned to safeguard his texts until he deemed them ready for circulation.

By the early thirteenth century, many European cities had a commercial book trade. The names of scribes, illuminators, parchment-makers and binders appear in tax records, though few names can be linked with surviving books. The first commercial illuminator in England documented from both archival sources and extant works is William de Brailes, who lived in Catte Street, Oxford, between 1230 and 1260. He specialized in de luxe books, and sometimes worked with other illuminators. In university cities (Paris, Bologna, Oxford), the book trade was largely governed by the university authorities. Booksellers had copies of set texts and rented them out to students and scribes for copying; the reliability of the text was a continual concern. Sometime before 1265, a Bolognese gentleman complained that, having given his son an allowance to study in Paris, the student had wasted his stipend on having his books 'monstrously decorated with gold letters' – the expensive decoration with gold and grotesques suggested by the verb '*babuinare*' pointed to more concern with play than work. Universities were the training grounds of those who became leading figures in church and secular government, and their expectations of what books should look like were developed there. If there is a standard look to medieval books (page layout, treatment of text with initials, capital initials, running titles, paragraph marks, etc.), we can attribute it to a standard maintained by a commercially-driven book trade in cities such as these.

Today such products can look magnificent, but we should probably not consider routine production in terms of artistic achievement. What is admirable is the effectiveness of the collective arrangements for guaranteeing standards. In discussing sculpture in fifteenth-century Germany, Michael Baxandall famously suggested that guild structures accounted for the routine and uninspired nature of production, and that inventiveness might flourish more easily in such places as Nuremberg, which was atypical of the larger cities in virtually banning the guilds. The same sort of issues arise if we look at the book trade and other commercial activities in Paris and other centres. If working practices are seen as a restraint on innovative production, it may be salutary to consider an anecdote concerning the French royal abbey of St Denis. In 1410 the exasperated monks were having problems with the professional Paris masons they employed, who were continually making images that pleased themselves rather than following the client's instructions: '[We] see everywhere workers amusing themselves with new and fancy styles.' Ways of working were entrenched in the trade. And yet the nature of what survives suggests that the demands of specific patrons could conjure forth some impressive works.

Even with archival sources, it can be difficult to know how many people worked in any one centre of the book trade. Richard and Mary Rouse state that twenty-four individuals would be a generous estimate for Paris in around 1300. Since production was family-based (and families might include the extended family and a few close friends and servants), the actual number of workers available might be more than the named individuals. For London in the 1470s, the names of some fifty people have been identified in archival sources whose trades were related to making books. As with other manufacturing activities, guilds emerged towards the end of the Middle Ages which established standards of production and rules for operating shops, and protected the trade hierarchy. Scribes in London had their own guilds or 'Misteries' by 1357, while illuminators had a separate one by 1400. In university towns the trade was under the control of university authorities. Paris had four sworn senior *libraires* and Oxford had licensed stationers as university officers. There were rules on such matters as training and apprenticeship (e.g. numbers and terms of employment), and for the ability to run a shop, but these are rarely mentioned. It was probably not easy for newcomers with no family links to set themselves up without buying in to the established network; working for the sovereign, which allowed trade regulations to be bypassed, could make life easier. The matter of stylistic change in these environments becomes particularly interesting.

Wealthy clients could employ producers directly. Richard de Bury (d.1345), author of a text on the joys of book collecting, recounts that he 'established relations with stationers and booksellers, not only in our own country but also in France, Germany and Italy, money going out in abundance to meet their demands'. He also said that he employed in his various manors a multitude of copyists and scribes, binders, correctors, illuminators and 'others who can work usefully in the service of books'. There could be no better testimony to the fact that books were not rare or marvellous commodities.

Even if we think in terms of a book trade, books could evidently be produced in different kinds of environment. In 1445, for example, the Oxford University stationer John Godson and the illuminator John Coveley were in dispute. The former was having difficulty in getting work back from the illuminator. The case came before the Chancellor's court, where it was decided that the illuminator, who lived in Oxford ('*infra muros ville Oxonie*'), should collect the books and the colours for illuminating them in person from the stationer, and deliver them back in good condition. His contract with the stationer was for one year, during which he was to work for no one else. The stationer gained the right to visit the illuminator's premises 'at opportune moments' to see how work was progressing. The stationer thus controlled both the issue of books and the pigments needed to illuminate them, and had the means of ensuring that his deadlines were met.

In 1481 a book dealer (*libraire*) of Avignon, Joachim of Rome, made a contract of employment with John Donat of Milan, a binder, scribe and illuminator. Donat was to live with his family in Joachim's shop, and to do work passed to him by Joachim at agreed rates of pay. For every

100 blue and red letters, Donat received one and a half *grossi* of Avignon currency; for red letters on their own, one *grossus* a hundred; for 1,000 blue and red paragraph marks, one and half *grossi*; and for 1,000 red paragraph marks, one *grossus*. Bindings were to be done at one and half *grossi* for large, and one *grossus* for small books. Donat was to pay Joachim four Florentine florins annually for use of the shop, and was allowed to make and sell on his own account books described as 'Matins, alphabet books, and the seven psalms' (i.e. books at the cheaper end of the market), provided this work did not delay completion of what Joachim gave him. Joachim wanted to have an illuminator and binder at his disposal, but was also prepared to let him work independently. In Nuremberg in the 1490s, Albrecht Dürer similarly allowed his journeymen to carry out independent commissions as time allowed.

Rather fuller anecdotal material survives in the case of André Le Musnier (d.1475), one of the four major university *libraires* of the University of Paris. Apart from archival sources, papers about him survived in the form of waste used to strengthen a binding (it was common in the late medieval and early modern periods to reuse in this way parchment from books and files no longer needed). A letter shows that Le Musnier employed at least one scribe who lived at some distance from Paris in a '*lieu plaisant*': the scribe wrote to report on work done, and to ask for more paper and for payment. This pattern – writing dispersed as a cottage industry, with the finishing and selling of books concentrated in commercial city centres – may have been common. An inventory of Le Musnier's goods show that he owned expensive equipment for grinding pigments (he doubtless supplied pigments to the illuminators he employed), and, remarkably, '*pourtraitures, histoires et vignettes*', or pictures and border ornament (*vignette* refers to border decoration). It was the bookseller, rather than the illuminator, who had a stock of compositions and designs, probably so that customers could choose the images and ornament desired in any book. The compositions were then distributed to illuminators to copy as directed.

Le Musnier inherited two apprentices from his father (who had at least three), bought two houses in the 1460s near the cathedral in Paris (the centre of the book trade there), and had a brother-in-law and descendants who were illuminators and a printer. He sold second-hand as well as new books, and had manuscript Books of Hours ready for sale – an important point, since, while the sheer number of Books of Hours produced in fifteenth-century France and the Low Countries suggests that they were produced speculatively (i.e. without any particular customer in mind), specific confirmation of this is rare. On one occasion, Le Musnier accepted work from the king, against university rules (in other cities those working for the king could be exempt from guild regulations, and there may have been an element of this in the case brought against Le Musnier by the university). André's business was carried on after his death by his widow, Thomasse, just as his father's business had been carried on by his mother, Jeannette. In all this, we see a pattern of work characteristic of the commercial world, one that served the nobility as much as the university and bourgeois classes.

Le Musnier was a forceful character (he appeared in court for beating up his brother-in-law), but much of what is known about him survives by chance. Rarely do members of the book trade speak directly to us, the outstanding exception being the Florentine book dealer Vespasiano da Bisticci (*c.*1422–98). Florence was a major centre of the book trade in Italy. There were shops around the Badia and elsewhere, but the scribes tended to be independent, employed on an *ad hoc* basis (many had other occupations such as priest or notary) and working at home. Vespasiano was the most successful of the *cartolai* – he was used by Cosimo de' Medici and his sons Piero and Giovanni in the 1460s to build up libraries (for the former, in late 1461, Vespasiano had to employ forty-five scribes to make a library of 200 books for the new Badia at Fiesole in twenty-two months) and by a host of other patrons. He supported the ambition of Federigo da Montefeltro to create the finest library since antiquity. The names of those he employed provide a roll-call of the best illuminators and scribes of fifteenth-century Italy. Retired from the 1480s, he wrote his memoirs, organizing his work as a biographical register of his clients, arranged by their rank – first popes, then a king (Alfonso of Aragon, King of Naples), a duke and other secular rulers, then cardinals, archbishops, bishops, statesmen (including John Tiptoft, Earl of Worcester; William Gray, Bishop of Ely; and Andrew Hollis, royal agent at the papal court) and writers. Details of their book-collecting activities are as interesting as the social prejudices the author reveals; he ended his days fearful of mob rule after the collapse of Medici power.

Of particular interest for the light it throws on the career of a working illuminator is the account of the interrogation of Jean Gillemer before a notoriously savage royal judge, Tristan l'Hermite, in 1471. Gillemer was accused of spying at a time when the French king Louis XI was at war with his brother Charles, Duke of Guyenne. The luckless Gillemer was arrested and imprisoned in Tours, since he was coming from Guyenne on his way to the Count of Maine, an ally of Charles. The illuminator was carrying various suspicious papers suggesting contact with the familiars of the Duke of Guyenne. The interrogation provides an astonishingly detailed picture of an artist who had to travel to seek commissions in regions not served by a permanent book trade. He had been to St Jean d'Angély (near Cognac), having heard that the wife of a certain Louis Baudet wanted to have a Book of Hours made and was willing to spend 25 *écus* (he had been informed of this by one of the lady's servants whom he had met near Poitiers some three months earlier). Baudet unfortunately was an official of the Duke of Guyenne. Gillemer had found work from one Johannes Demeré, who had written out a psalter (Demeré turned out to be a scribe employed by the Duke of Guyenne). Gillemer then went to Bordeaux to have bound a Book of Hours he had sold to Antoine, a *valet de chambre* of the duke. Gillemer's journey to Le Mans was to get full payment for illuminated books made earlier for the Count of Maine – he protested that he had no missive from the Duke of Guyenne.

L'Hermite was curious about papers discovered on Gillemer. Some were charms – one had been bought in a tavern near Poitiers and when worn around the neck was held to cure toothache; another could be used to gain the love of a woman; others were psalms and prayers, one of them bought in Paris and another copied from a book in the church of St Hilaire de Poitiers, translated into French by a friendly priest. One paper was a picture of Christ bought in Brussels which when enlarged sixteen times would supposedly give the actual proportions of Christ's body. A piece of writing with crosses had been bought when Gillemer was in Lyons after returning from Lombardy. Most interesting in throwing light on working practices was a list of names annotated with days of the week. Gillemer explained that he had brought together, some three years earlier in Poitiers, a group of *serviteurs* to help him 'exercise his profession of illuminator'. They had refused to help him properly. He approached one Brother Jean Boussin, who extracted advice from a book of astrology. The suspect paper merely gave a list of the days of the week on which, according to the stars, it would be best to ask Charles, Simon, Pierre, Guillaume, Jean and Etienne to provide work.

Gillemer's talents were evidently not as a team leader, and were perhaps best employed in private commissions. It has been remarked that the work of the Master of Charles de France, an anonymous illuminator employed by the Duke of Guyenne, shows awareness of Italian fashions. He was a highly original illuminator, whose products show extraordinary finesse and sense of detail in carefully structured landscapes, and he worked for various noble patrons throughout France. Were it possible to link him with Gillemer or his like, this would locate originality outside the environment of the established book trade.

Why are these details about the circumstances of making books an appropriate introduction to looking at illuminated manuscripts? Sources make it clear that the production of books was a collaborative enterprise involving co-operation between different crafts: parchment-maker, scribe, illuminator and binder, together with, in many cases, a bookdealer who took orders from clients and oversaw the making of the final article. Book production was a business activity involving a multitude of skills; an illuminated page was the work of a variety of people, whose contributions can be discerned like a series of archaeological layers. In the past, it was fashionable to talk of workshops in which an illuminator controlled the making of a book, but it is difficult to discover such things from archival sources. The experience of Gillemer in Poitiers indicates that teams might be brought together for specific enterprises, and the situation in Paris points to systematic subcontracting and co-operative working practices. Surviving manuscripts show that there were good illuminators and less good illuminators, but it is not always clear whether the latter were incompetent imitators of the former, or less effective practitioners of a shared style. Such questions have emerged in the study of objects as diverse as silverware and furniture, once confidently attributed to individual master craftsmen and now seen as the products of trades that provided elements put together at the point of sale by an entrepreneur, who might himself have been a silversmith or furniture-maker but whose main skill was on the business side.

2

On Scripts and Scribes

Scripts changed throughout the Middle Ages. Developments in letter shapes and ways of writing were related to the evolving needs of government, university study, scholarship and the development of vernacular literatures. One of the legacies of Charlemagne's rule in the decades before and after 800 was a standardized script used throughout Europe. As part of ecclesiastical reform, biblical and liturgical texts were improved and standardized, while great energies were spent in gathering together and writing out classical texts (we owe our knowledge of many Roman writers today to Carolingian manuscripts). As part of this activity, a new script was developed, today called Carolingian minuscule. It was developed in such places as Corbie and Tours – at the latter monastery it was used for the series of great Bibles made to be sent to institutions elsewhere. The script was gradually adopted all over Europe; it began to be used in England from the tenth century. A late version of this kind of script is written in a style used in the area around Rome, and at the monastery of Farfa, in the late eleventh century (plate1). It presents a rather square version of the Carolingian script but retains the latter's spacious clarity. It is paired with a version of ancient Roman capitals known as rustic capitals, as were the best demonstrations of the script in Carolingian times.

1 Carolingian minuscule script, with initial, from a Lectionary. Italy (Farfa or near Rome), late 11th century.

It was a small, often more compressed, version of this script that was to be used in continental Europe (and after 1066 increasingly in Britain) for the great task of stocking the libraries of the monasteries founded in such profusion in the eleventh and twelfth centuries. It also provided the model for the script in which commentaries on the Bible were written in the margins next to the larger text of the Bible itself, by which time we see clearly the diagonal hairline serifs showing that the pen was held at an angle (plate 2), a portent of the Gothic scripts that were about to emerge. Scripts like this characterize the

Gothic for us today. By the end of the Middle Ages, rather abstract versions were regularly used for liturgical texts, and the biting of letters (i.e. when part of a letter is fused to the next one) can make them difficult to read for those who do not know the text in advance (plate 3). In Italy, the Gothic scripts that emerged in the thirteenth century were distinctively rounded, both in versions developed for canon and civil law texts and those used for liturgical purposes (plate 4).

Gothic scripts were time-consuming to produce, especially those for large books that were designed to be seen from a distance by, for example, a choir or officiating priest. Cursive hands emerged in the eleventh and twelfth centuries for charters and informal writing. Formal versions of these scripts were promoted into hands suitable for books. In England, a distinctive book hand emerged based on cursive scripts. An example of 1340 (plate 5) shows cursive origins, with splayed ascenders, a *d* with an ascender looped backwards, a round, o-like *s* as well as the tall *s*, and a deep *r* that cuts below the line and joins the next letter without the pen leaving the surface of the parchment. Formal scripts of this kind came to include elements of both cursive and formal text hands, and are thus known as 'bastard hands'. Widely used in the fifteenth century, for literary and other purposes, the script was also known as 'Burgundian letters' – the literary works made for the dukes of Burgundy in the fifteenth century were in scripts of this kind (plate 6).

Scripts carried messages about the status of the texts they transmitted. Formal Gothic scripts had authority and were not used for the same purposes as the cursive scripts that appear from the twelfth century. In the fifteenth century semi-official texts such as Books of Hours began to be written in the 'bastard' scripts used for literary works and not automatically in traditional Gothic scripts. From the 1460s some in the Low Countries began to be written in the rounded Gothic script associated with Italy, while from the end of the century scribes might be called on to employ the most advanced Roman scripts in imitation of fine printing (plate 7).

The great innovation of the fifteenth century was the development of Roman letter shapes imitating Carolingian scripts. Petrarch in the 1370s expressed discontent with common scripts. In Florence, Chancellor Coluccio Salutati (1331–1406), himself experimenting with clearer letter forms in his own script, encouraged the efforts of Poggio Bracciolini (1380–1459) to develop a new script based on the tenth- and eleventh-century manuscripts in Carolingian scripts which they encountered in their search for classical texts. In fact, all aspects of early books were imitated, from ruling (hard-point ruling was revived to replace pencil or ink), quiring (ten folios rather than eight for each gathering), and page layout (spacious margins with regular proportions). Initially developed in the spirit of antiquarian revival, the script involved the reintroduction of the a-e ligature (*æ*), the long *s* (like an *f*), and the ampersand (*&*). But the letter shapes became widely accepted during the fifteenth century (by 1430 professional scribes in Florence and then Italy regularly used the new humanistic scripts for copies of the Latin classics) and are those we use today (plate 8). A cursive version – italic – was invented by Bracciolini's associate Niccolò Niccoli (1364/5–1437) and was linked throughout Europe from this time with humanistic education (plate 9). At first confined to circles of scholars, many of whom were also prominent

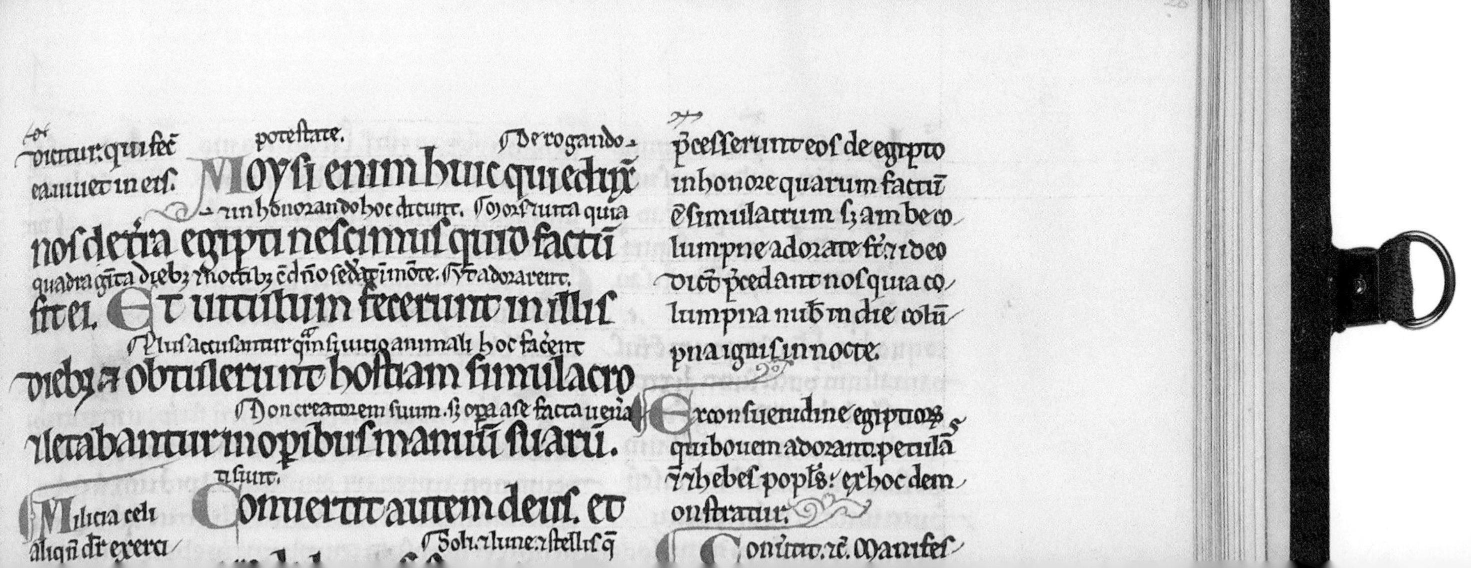

2 (opposite) Proto-Gothic script, from a glossed Acts of the Apostles. Paris, third quarter of the 12th century.

3 (top right) Gothic script, from a Psalter. England, mid-15th century.

4 (right) Italian Gothic script, from a Missal. Italy, first half of the 14th century.

5 (below) Current 'Anglicana' script, from an inventory of the armour, arms and other goods of Sir John Molyns, at Thames Ditton, Surrey and elsewhere. England, 1340.

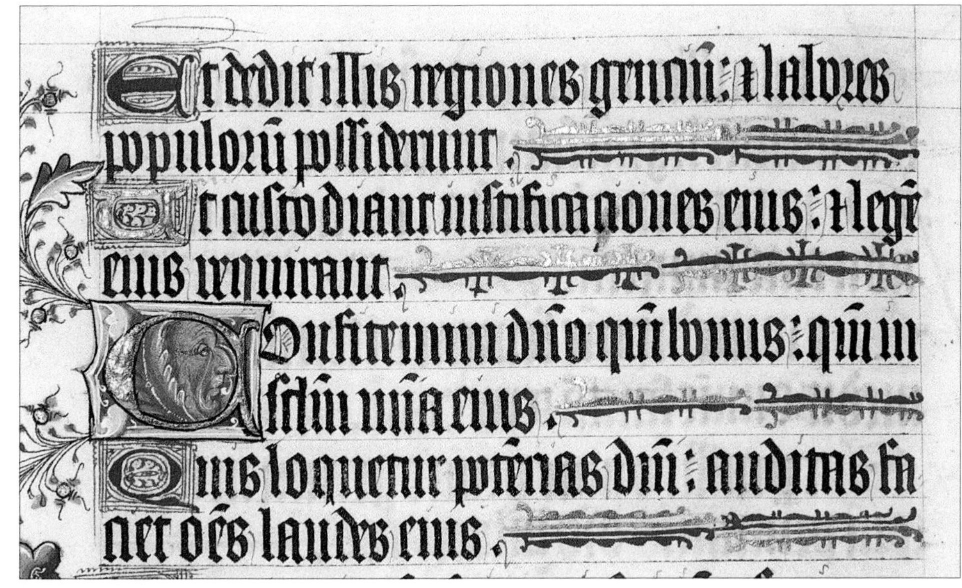

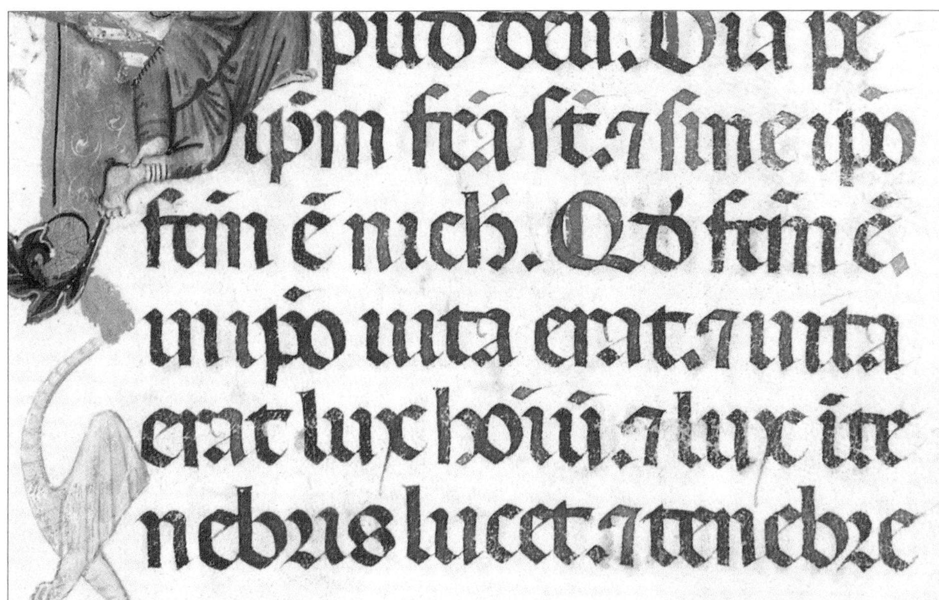

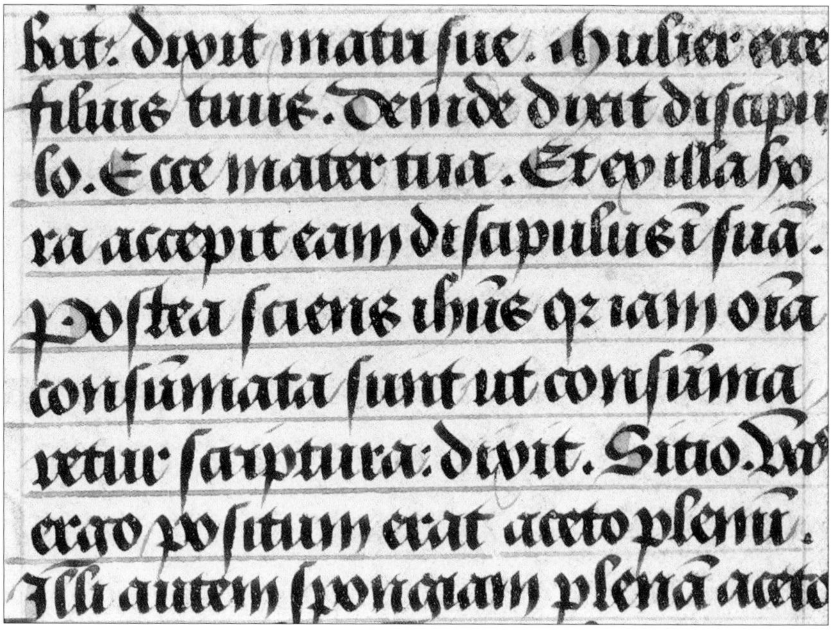
hic: dixit matri sue. Mulier ecce
filius tuus. Deinde dixit discipu
lo. Ecce mater tua. Et ex illa ho
ra accepit eam discipulus in sua.
Postea sciens ihesus quia iam omnia
consummata sunt ut consumma
retur scriptura: dixit. Sitio. Uas
ergo positum erat aceto plenum.
Illi autem spongiam plenam aceto

6 'Bastard' script, from a Book of Hours (the 'Playfair Hours'). France (Rouen), *c.*1480.

bureaucrats in church and state, it eventually became the standard hand in administrative chanceries and even up-market prayer books. Printed versions of the new italic script emerged in the late fifteenth century, and a European standard for the *cancellaresca* appeared with writing books published in 1522 and 1524 by Ludovico Arrighi and Giovantonio Tagliente.

Unlike such activities as illuminating or binding, knowledge of how to write was spread widely throughout society in the late Middle Ages. Many priests turned to writing to make money. The ability to write was assumed in certain religious orders. The Carthusians, as we have seen, were obliged to write – 'Those who can write and are unwilling to do so will be deprived of wine on the orders of the prior', stated their statutes in 1259. Different scripts were attached to different kinds of activity. In London in 1357, the professional association of scribes, the 'Mistery' or guild, was for those who specialized in either 'court letter' (i.e. scripts for administrative purposes) or 'text letter' (formal hands for books). By 1373 writers of court letter and text letter had their own 'Misteries'. Skill in writing was always admired. Professional writers could supply a variety of scripts at different prices (some were quicker to write and thus cheaper). A scribe named Pierre Colin writing near Geneva in 1469 left a note at the back of the book listing his charges for different scripts (how much writing you got for each sum is not stated): 5 *gros* for register letters (*littera registri*), 8 *gros* for essay letters (*littera de essay*), 1 *sous* for genre letters (*littera de genere*). It also provides other information about prices: the book cost 5 *sous* 10 *gros*, of which the parchment cost 3 *sous*, the binding 1 *sous*, the writing 1 *sous*, the box in which it was to be kept 9 *gros*, and the 'illumination' (in this case the colour given to the initials) 1 *gros*.

This scribe's bill throws light on the whole matter of the prices of books. It is, of course, difficult to estimate the actual value of Pierre Colin's bill. It shows the relative expense of a particular work that received minimal illumination: the support (parchment – possibly ruled parchment) cost over half of the total bill. Paper was increasingly used from the fourteenth century (though the first paper mill reported in England dates from the 1490s), meaning that books could be much cheaper. One parchment skin in 1500, it has been calculated, cost the equivalent of 100 sheets of good linen paper. And yet for certain classes of book, particularly service books and Books of Hours, the use of parchment seems to have been the norm (only in the age of printing was paper to become the predominant support for the latter). One set of calculations, for Paris in the early fifteenth century, indicates that, for the kind of books owned by lawyers for example, it took six and a half days' wages of a notary in royal service to buy a second-hand book, or eleven and a half days' wages for a new book (these notaries can be compared to modern senior civil servants or company directors).

Liturgical books, especially those designed for display as well as function, might represent vast amounts of financial investment. The Missal commissioned by Nicolas Litlyngton, Abbot of Westminster Abbey, in 1383–84 was made in the abbey itself for use there. It cost over £36; the scribe, a layman named Thomas Preston, worked at it for two years (there were just over 680 pages, the text with an average of 30 lines a page), receiving £4 as well as free board and lodging and clothes to the value of £1; the parchment cost £4 6s 8d. The major expense was the series of fifty-six historiated initials and miniatures: at £22 0s 3d, they cost 7s 10d each, while the

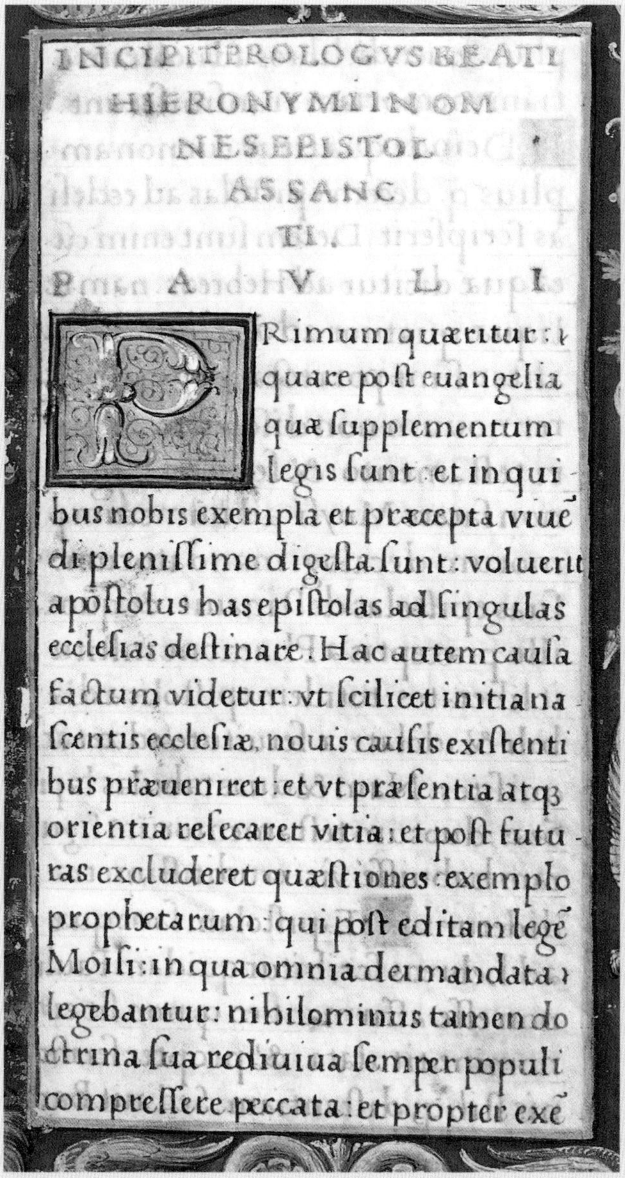

7 (left) Roman script, from the Pauline Epistles (the 'Leuville Epistes'). France (?Tours or Loire Valley), *c.*1520–30.

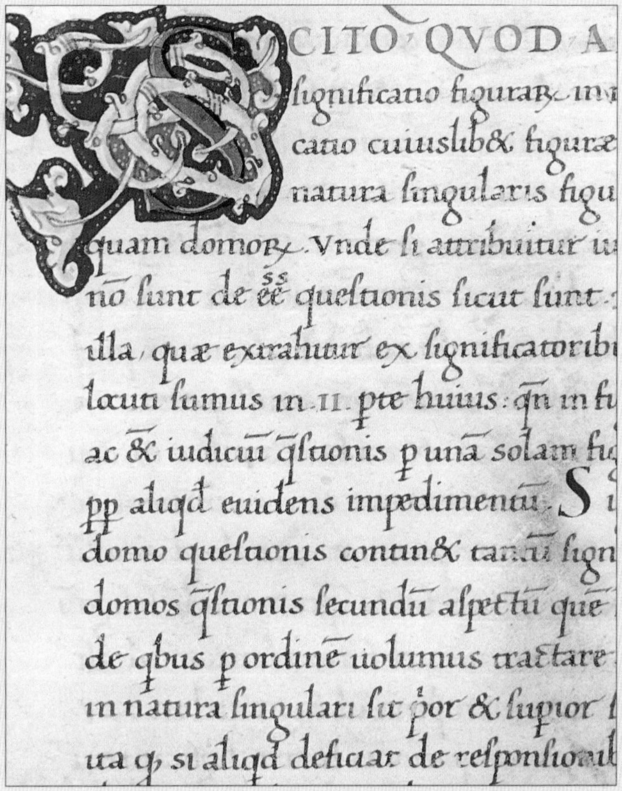

8 (above) Humanistic script, from a 12th-century treatise on divination and geomancy, 'Ars completa geomantiae', written by Bartolomeo Sanvito. Italy, *c.*1460–70.

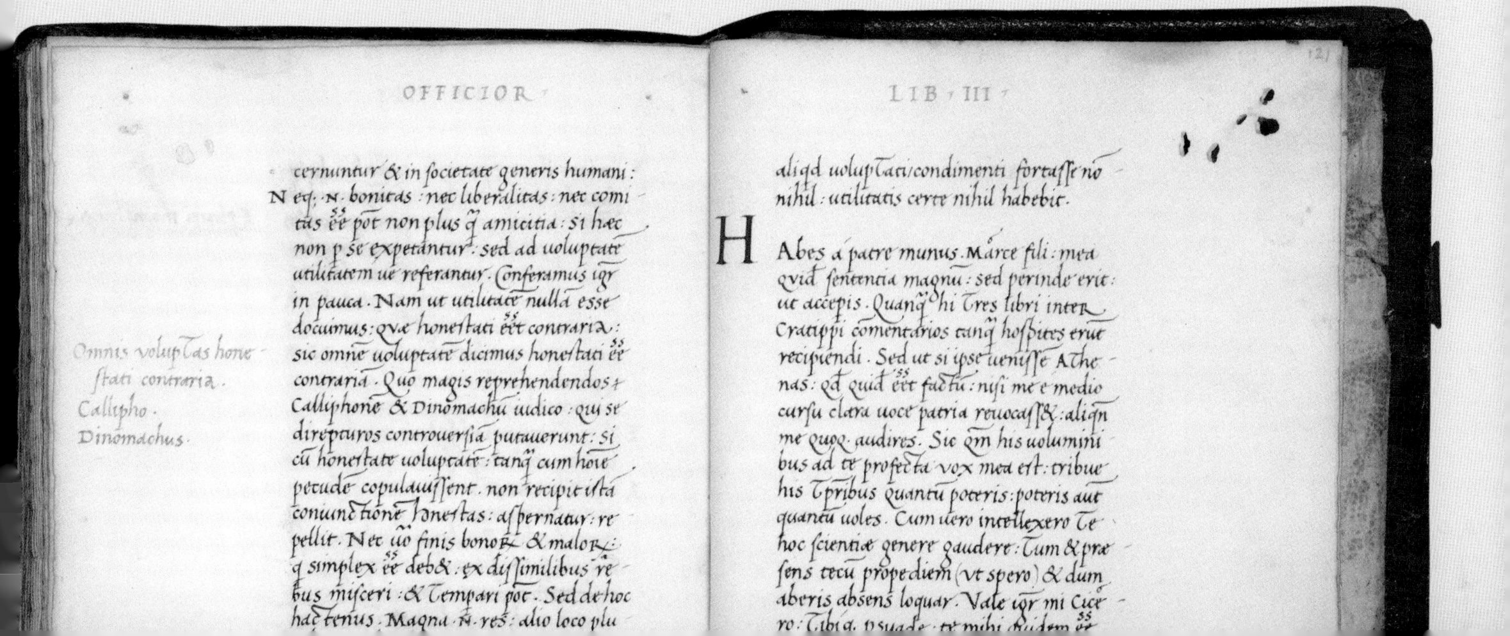

9 (below) Humanistic cursive (Italic) script, from a copy of Cicero, *De officiis*, written by Bartolomeo Sanvito.Italy (Rome), 1495.

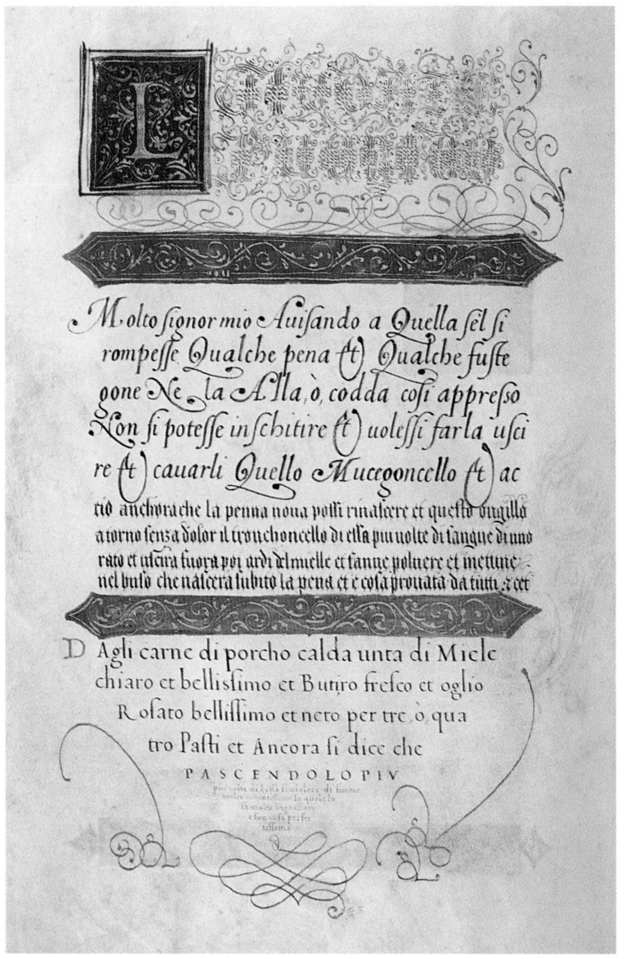

central image, the Crucifixion, cost 10s. The team responsible for the illumination consisted of a chief decorator and three figure painters (Sandler, 1986, vol. II, pp. 172–74). This was a substantial investment, and the result was a quite outstanding work. At the same time, a second-hand university textbook might cost as little as 10s, and a major text such as Augustine's *City of God* between £1 and £2. To give an indication of what such sums meant, it is worth noticing that a master mason, perhaps the equivalent of a major building contractor today, might earn up to £10 a year.

Archival sources sometimes show us the conditions in which scribes operated. In a contract of 1399 at Dijon, one Jean de Molin, '*escripvain*' but here acting as an entrepreneur, subcontracted the actual writing of a copy of the *Roman de la Rose* to a scribe who was a cleric, Jean Denisot, to be written following a model of script supplied. The work was to be finished in three months, and Denisot was to be supplied with parchment ruled for the purpose (ruled parchment was apparently a commodity that could be bought). We can calculate that the text was written at just over 250 lines a day. Although such calculations are imprecise, this is not far from the figure calculated as an average for Paris in the early fourteenth century by one scholar, who arrived at the figure of just under three folios (i.e. six pages, perhaps of forty-five lines each) a day. On other occasions, the scribe might additionally undertake decoration, and be supplied with colours by the person ordering the work. Teaching might also be one of his activities – a few advertising posters survive from the late Middle Ages, of which one of the most impressive is that of Master Johann von Hagen (first half of the fifteenth century). He offered training in a variety of scripts 'such as are now used in the courts of various lords' ('*prout nunc scribitur in curiis dominorum*') (plate 11). A writing master of Erfurt in around 1500 left an advertisement in both German and Latin offering to teach five different scripts: legal cursive (*notula curiensis*), square book script (*textus quadratus*), round book script (*textus rotundus*), small book script (*textus abscissus*) and also *floritura et illuminatura* (i.e. decorative elements such as paragraph marks, ornamental initials and flourishing that readers expected in properly written and finished books). A master of this kind tried in 1492 to nail his notice '*pro introductione artis scribendi*' ('for an introduction to the art of writing') on the door of Rouen Cathedral, but the cathedral canons apparently preferred having indulgences (documents allowing the faithful to contribute financially to a worthy cause and thus gain remission of time in Purgatory) rather than commercial advertisements on their doors.

What writing masters offered were probably advanced courses in the skills necessary for professional advancement in chanceries and other government departments. When, around 1507–9, a scribe from the abbey of Saints Ulrich and Afra in Augsburg, Leonhard Wagner, compiled a dazzling display of samples of one hundred named scripts, '*Proba centum scripturarum*', he dedicated it to the Holy Roman Emperor Maximilan I, who would have been aware of the uses of this skill. Although Wagner, as a monk, may not have had to rely on his skill to earn his wages, the scribe Francesco Moro of Pozzoveggiano, described as a 'priest of Padua' by a contemporary, probably did. His writing book of *c.*1560 (plate 10) showed a dazzling array of scripts and was dedicated to Lorenzo Ridolfi, possibly the brother of Nicolo Ridolfi de' Medici (d.1550), made a cardinal in 1517 by the Medici pope, Leo X.

10 (opposite) Samples of scripts, from the writing manual by Francesco Moro of Pozzoveggiano. Italy, *c.*1560.

11 (right) Samples of scripts, from the writing sheet of Johann von Hagen. Germany (Lower Saxony), *c.*1400.

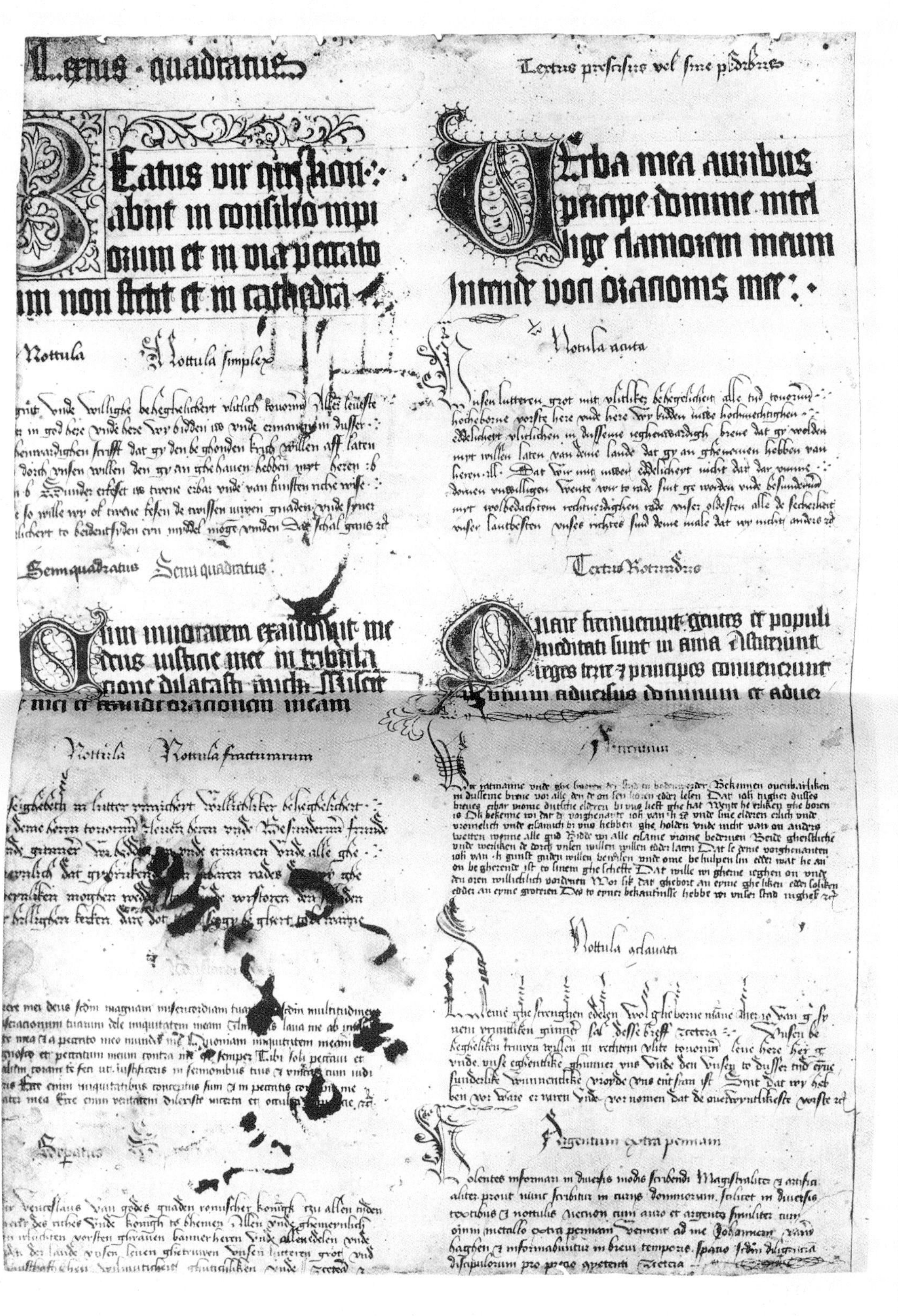

Textus quadratus

Beatus vir qui non abiit in consilio impiorum et in via peccatorum non stetit et in cathedra

Textus prescissus vel sine pedibus

Verba mea auribus percipe domine intellige clamorem meum intende voci orationis mee

Nottula simplex

Notula acuta

Semiquadratus

Cum invocarem exaudivit me deus iusticie mee in tribulatione dilatasti michi Miserere mei et exaudi orationem meam

Textus Rotundus

Quare fremuerunt gentes et populi meditati sunt inania Astiterunt reges terre et principes convenerunt in unum adversus dominum et adver

Nottula fractumurum

3

Decorative Initials

Professionally-made books used decorative initials to signal the major divisions of a text. There was usually a hierarchy of initials within any book to designate sections, chapters, paragraphs and other breaks. The initials were added either by the scribe or, increasingly in the later Middle Ages, by a specialist, in spaces left blank by the scribe. The important initials might be historiated (i.e. with a figurative picture, *istoire* being the term for a story) or decorated, while the lesser initials were made up of coloured letters on coloured or gold grounds, often with flourishing in ink of a contrasting colour.

A group of initials in the V&A collection exemplifies the variety of styles common in twelfth-century manuscripts. A number come from manuscripts that were apparently once in the library of the abbey of Pontigny, near Auxerre. The most humble initials show a sequence of green, red, blue and yellow – colours characteristic of the minor decoration of manuscripts from this kind of environment, quite different from the red and blue that became the norm from the thirteenth century (plate 12). The ornament of major initials is based on swirling stems that spiral around the letter shape, with leafy terminals, shoots and large acanthus leaves displayed frontally to reveal radiating sprays. For one (plate 13), the *B* comprises a panel for the vertical stroke and interlaced stems that recall the strapwork of Carolingian initials, while the bowls frame spiral stems that issue from dragon mouths intertwined with leaves. Red hatching marks out the elements of the letter shape, and white stems with green shading outline areas of plain blue, green, red and yellow, the whole being on a yellow ground unbounded by any framing line. In another initial, white stems with coloured or white leafy terminals mark out both the letter shape, *H*, and the spirals that end in one partially closed and one fully open acanthus leaf. This is an inhabited initial, since there are two huntsmen and dogs chasing a hare in the thicket of ornament, the man with the drawn bow and arrow marvellously poised as he searches out his prey (plate 14). Another Pontigny manuscript (plate 15), a copy of Gratian's compendium of Canon Law, has initials of a rather different kind. The colour scheme is based on green, slate-grey and orange ochre; the letter-shape is picked out in the orange ochre, while coloured leaves here and in the tail that stretches to the margin lie on a deep green ground firmly bounded by a line. The stylistic differences suggest that the illuminators involved were trained in different traditions.

Initials such as these were used for the patristic and other texts that European monasteries needed for their libraries at the time of the great expansion of Benedictine orders from the eleventh century. These were generally working books, and decorative initials were often the major part of the ornament. In early thirteenth-century Germany, we can find the same reliance on spirals of white stems as the basis of ornament. An initial *R* (plate 16) is made up of such stems with leafy sprouts, with the curved elements of the letter shape represented as dragons' wings (in one case the corresponding biting head mistakenly attached as a tail). Spiralling stems of this kind were regularly associated with a dragon, a decorative device used throughout Europe (plate 17).

Another kind of twelfth-century initial, commonly used in France and England as a secondary initial and recently termed an 'arabesque' initial, was a simple pattern in one

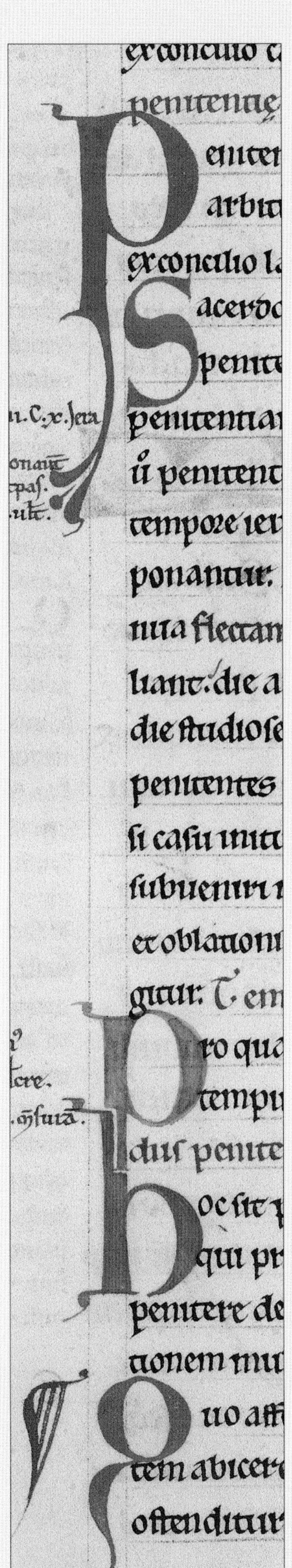

12 (left) Initials from a copy of St Gregory's *Moralia in Job*. France, 12th century.

13 (top right) Letter *B* from a copy of St Gregory's *Moralia in Job*. France, 12th century.

14 (bottom right) Letter *H* from a copy of St Gregory's *Moralia in Job*. France, 12th century.

15 (left) Letter *Q* from a copy of Gratian's *Decretum*. France, 12th century.

16 (below) Letter *R* from a choirbook. Germany, late 12th century.

17 (right) Letter with dragon ornament, from a Psalter, perhaps made for a Cistercian abbey. Germany (?Rhineland), mid-13th century.

18 (far right) Arabesque initial, from the St Maurice d'Agaune Evangelistary-Missal. Switzerland (?St Maurice-en-Valais), late 12th century.

or two colours. An example comes from a manuscript probably made for the abbey of St Maurice d'Agaune in Switzerland (plate 18). Initials in a thirteenth-century manuscript, made for a monastery in the south of France, use coloured inks to create exotic floral shapes and flowing antennae that spread into the margin (plate 19).

These decorative initials marked significant divisions of the text by making the heading memorable. The best way to do this was to show a picture related to the subject of the text – a standard method for the more expensive Bibles produced in the thirteenth century. The magnificent Glazier-Rylands Bible produced in Hainaut in 1260–70 had historiated initials of this kind (plate 20). Here, the arch of the *A* is made up of an elongated winged dragon that listens cheekily to Solomon as he sits with a group of Jews in inverted-funnel hats (the pose of the dragon is found in other manuscripts and thus was perhaps not a spontaneous joke by the illuminator). The letter shape is incidental to the image; during the next century, historiated initials such as these were frequently replaced by square miniatures integrated into the width of the text column. Such initials functioned as index markers in Bibles and the great liturgical books needed for church services. A late thirteenth-century example of the latter, from the church in Arezzo, shows the choir's part for Mass on Easter Sunday marked by a scene of the three Maries at the tomb beneath Christ in Majesty, blessing in the manner of a Byzantine icon (plate 21). In Italy, compact historiated initials, neatly integrated into the first few lines of a text arranged in two columns on the page, became standard for legal texts, Bibles and liturgical works. They often had knotted stems protruding down the margins to end with a spiral; the colours (deep blue, slate grey, red and orange) denote a scheme first established in manuscripts made in Bologna (plate 22).

Some types of initial had an extraordinary longevity. Simple initials in alternating red and blue, with contrasting flourished decoration by pen in blue and red (letters in gold and blue with contrasting flourishing are also common), can be found over several centuries. The penwork flourishing was later developed in all parts of Europe. A common type, termed 'champie initials' (*littere champide*) in one rare manuscript, comprised simple letter shapes in burnished gold with a red or blue infill on a ground of blue or red, each ground enlivened with highlighting in delicately traced white lines (plate 23). 'Puzzle initials' (*littere duplices* or *littere partite*) have the

letter shape made up in red and blue with an irregular line left blank to separate the colours, the whole decorated with penwork flourishing (plates 24 and 25). All these initials emerged in the later twelfth century in northern France, especially Paris, and England, and represent a scheme of design that was taken up by the secular book trade. They became what the literate, educated classes of Europe accepted as the standard in well-finished books.

A rather later arrival was the initial (and associated decorative scheme) based on a three-pointed leaf, often called vine-leaf initial, widely used from the thirteenth century and common up to the second half of the fifteenth. In this scheme, three-pointed leaves in blue and red or orange-red, shaded with white, grow out of a coiled stem within or around the letter shape, which is in red or blue with white highlighting. The interior and exterior ground is of burnished gold or has a gold element (plate 26). This kind of initial gave way to a variation using grey foliage on a red ground for the letter-shape, on a ground of brushed gold with semi-naturalistic flowers and berries (plate 27). Versions were used for the illuminated printed Books of Hours that issued from Paris presses from the late 1480s. In both manuscripts and printed books, they were rivalled towards the end of the century by simple initials where the letter shape was simply painted in brushed gold on a monochrome coloured ground (this was evidently a cheaper way of making the text properly readable).

These initials – ivy-leaf and grey foliage on a red ground – were widely used in France, Flanders and England. They contrast with those used in German-speaking lands. In Holland an initial with a bulbous flower in the centre was characteristic (plate 28).

The provision of illuminated initials was doubtless one of the chores of junior members of a production team and, like preparing and applying pigments, was part of learning the illuminator's trade. In Avignon a three-year contract established in 1455 concerned the apprenticeship of one François Bequat to Master Henri Feynaud, 'illuminator of books' (*illuminator librorum*). Apart from domestic chores and fetching wine from the local tavern, François was to learn the '*ars illuminature librorum*' 'according to the usual plan and steps in teaching that art' ('*secundum cursus et gradus communes docendi in illa arte*'). It was stressed that he was to honour his master in all circumstances, and above all, reveal the 'secrets' of his trade to nobody. After apprenticeship, you could earn your living as an illuminator, supplying initials being one of the essential skills. The illuminator Jean Donat in Avignon, who in 1481 agreed to supply simple initials to his employer for a fixed rate (see p. 10), was a subordinate figure in the book trade in that he did not have his own premises. When the artist Jan van Eyck was

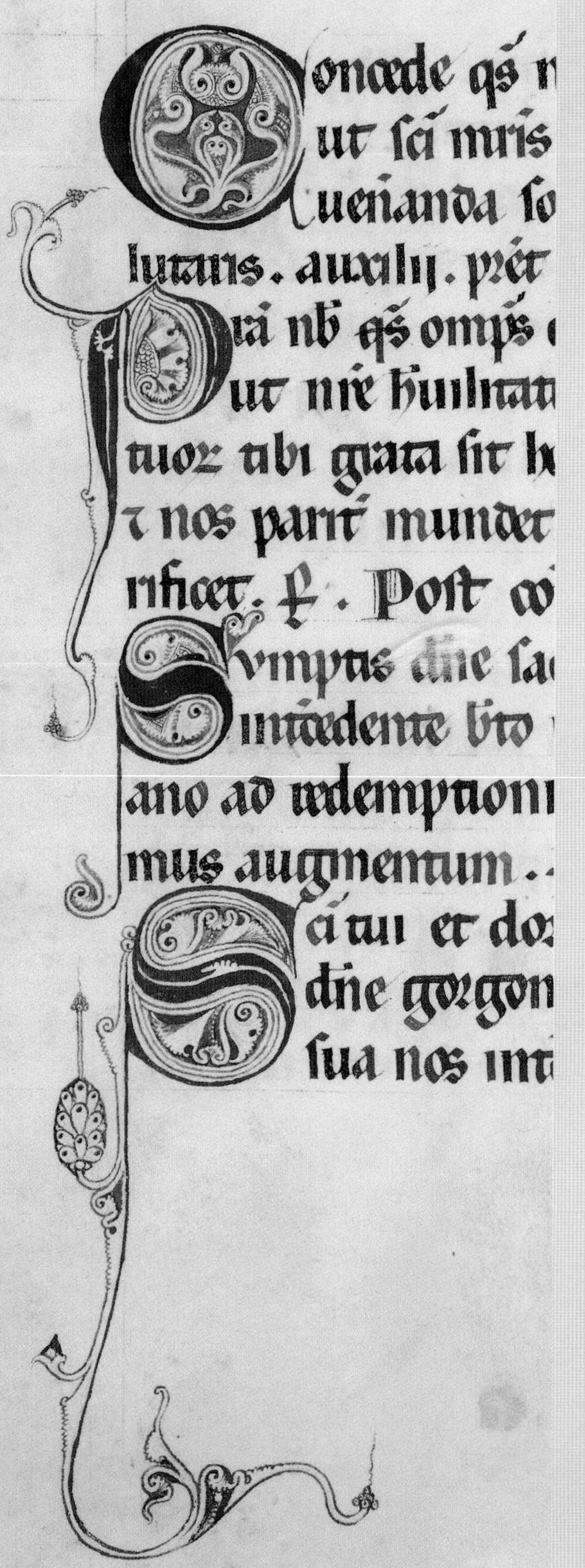

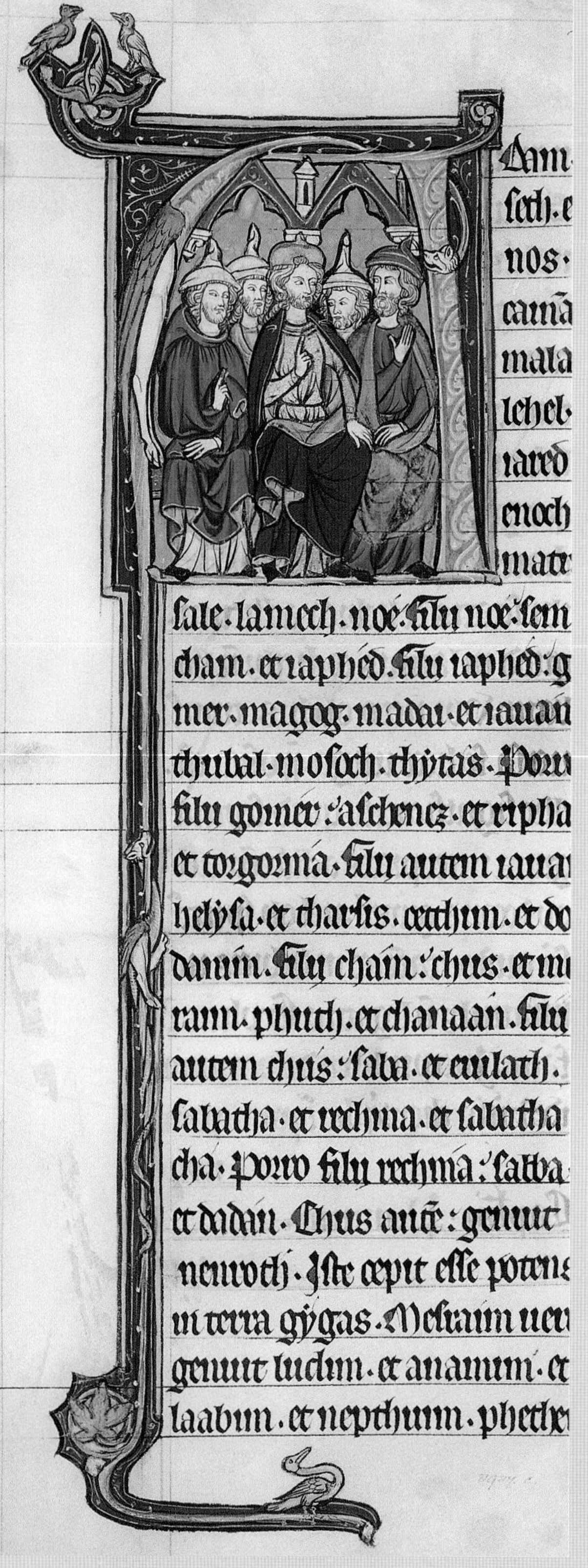

19 (opposite left) Initials from a monastic Missal. Southern France, 13th century.

20 (opposite right) Historiated initial *A* (Solomon addressing a group of Jews) from the Glazier-Rylands Bible. Low Countries (Hainaut), 1260–70.

21 (right) Historiated initial *R*, from a Gradual. Italy (Arezzo), late 13th century.

paid by the ducal treasurer in 1439 for supplying such initials, he was receiving money for illumination done by a subcontractor.

If designing initials was one of the basic training disciplines for apprentices, then the 'Göttingen Model Book', a manual of *c.*1460 (with another copy in Berlin) that describes how to paint a standard kind of fifteenth-century German initial, creates something of a problem. It describes how to execute the commonest of all initials found in German manuscripts. The initials have outline letter shapes containing foliate designs picked out on a dark ground, and large acanthus leaves that swirl around a rod as ornament. Why was a manual needed for such a common initial? One explanation is that the volume of work created by the advent of multiple copies from the printing press meant that extra – untrained – hands had to be recruited and trained (plates 29 and 30, and see plate 104).

A rather different ornamental repertoire appears in fifteenth-century Italian manuscripts, where the white-vine initial was developed to accompany the first humanist manuscripts. Like the script, it represents a version of tenth-century models. By the 1430s it was being used in the book trade, and not long afterwards it lost its humanist associations with classical texts and was adopted for literary and devotional works (plate 31). A form associated initially with manuscripts done for the Gonzaga court at Mantua in the mid-fifteenth century contained a knotted interlace (plates 32 and 33), a design also used for ornament tooled on to bindings. As part of the archaeologically-inspired antiquarian movement associated with Felice Feliciano, Mantegna and others, faceted initials in imitation of Roman inscriptions became fashionable from the 1460s (plate 34). They form a complete contrast to traditional designs such as that found on a choirbook of 1492 from Verona, in which the leafy acanthus surrounds a yellow ring within which there might be ornament or a picture (plate 35).

22 (left) Historiated initial (Ahaziah falling from a tower; IV Kings), from a Bible. Northern Italy, *c.*1275–1300.

23 (below) Minor initials, from the Zouche Hours. Southern Low Countries (?Bruges), 1470–80.

24 (opposite, left) 'Puzzle' initial from the St Maurice d'Agaune Evangelistary-Missal. Switzerland (?St Maurice-en-Valais), late 12th century.

25 (opposite, right) 'Puzzle' initials from a Bible. Northern Low Countries (nunnery of Diepenveen), 1450–53.

26 (opposite, below) Initial from the St Denis Missal. France (Paris), *c.*1350.

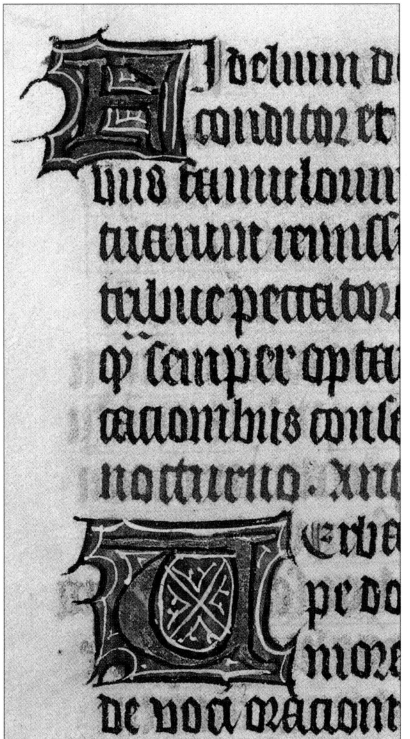

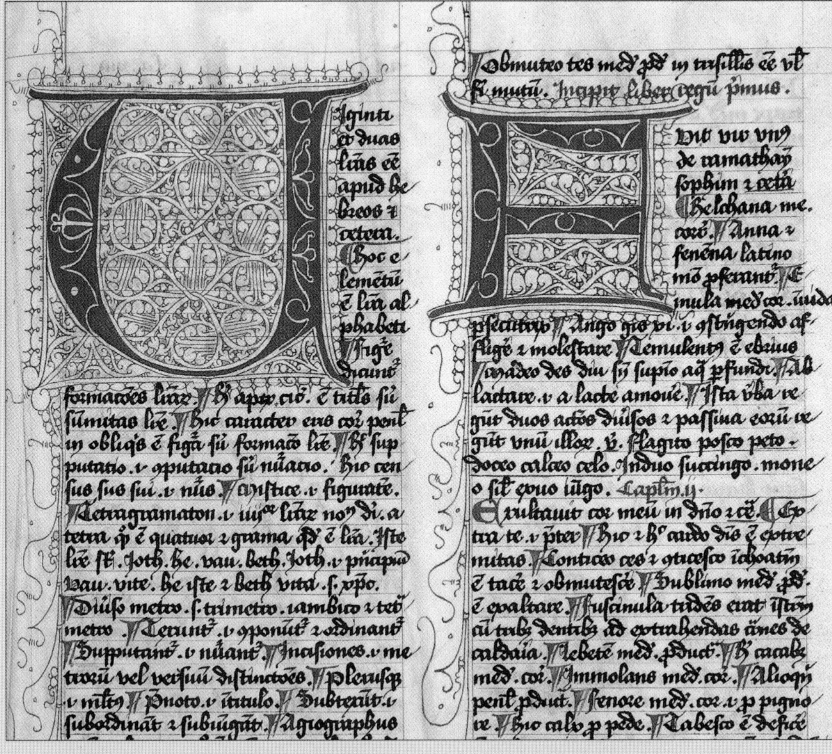

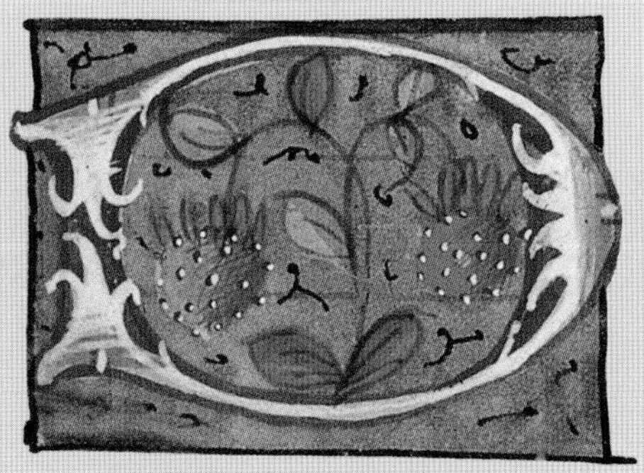

27 (left) Initial from the 'Playfair Hours'. France (Rouen), *c.*1480.

28 (right) Initial from a Book of Hours. Northern Low Countries, *c.*1470–80.

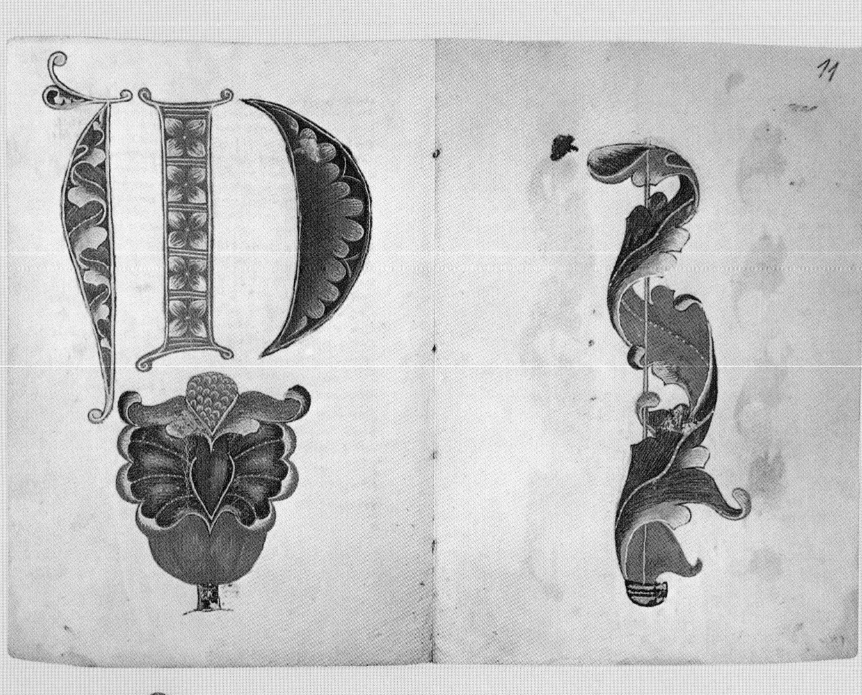

29 (above) Page from the Göttingen Model Book. Germany (Middle Rhineland), second half of the 15th century.

30 (left) Cut-out initial *A*. Germany (Middle Rhineland), *c.*1460.

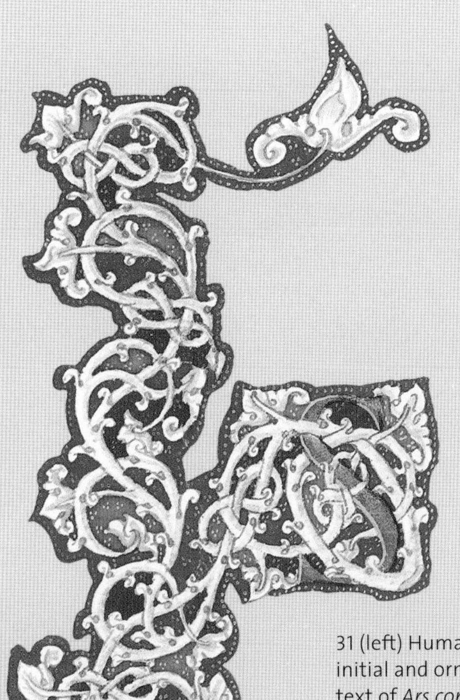

31 (left) Humanistic white-vine initial and ornament, from a text of *Ars completa geomantiae*. Italy (?Rome), *c.*1460–70.

32 (above left) Initial from a copy of Lucan, *Pharsalia*. Italy (possibly Mantua), 1471.

33 (above) Initial, from a copy of Palladius, *De agricultura*. Italy, *c.*1460–70.

34 (left) Faceted initial *Q*, from a copy of Petrarch, *Sonnets and Triumphs*. Italy (?Padua), *c.*1463–64.

35 (above) Historiated initial *E* with an image of St Zeno. Italy (Verona), 1492.

4

Ornamental Flourishing

Initials were often associated with ornament that sprayed into margins. One type of ornament, systematically used in illumination from the thirteenth century, was clearly a specialist activity: pen-flourishing in red, blue or other colours (purple ink was favoured in the fifteenth century) could be carried out by the person responsible for initials. In its simplest form it was an economical way of marking a division in a book, as in a copy of the Acts of the Apostles done just after 1200 in Bologna, which reflects the layout of works produced for the university there.

Simple flourishes shoot into the margin like fireworks, sometimes with a comic face or grotesque (plate 36). Attempts to distinguish regional traditions have been less successful than efforts to identify hands of different pen-flourishers in the same manuscript (see Rouse, 2000, vol. II, plates 62 and 63). The flourishing in some later Italian Bibles has become a major decorative element, with designs of compact ornament and energetic strokes (plate 37). Another version shows a dense pattern that sits more emphatically on the page (plate 38). In Paris an illuminator named Jacques Maci, who specialized in work of this kind, was active in the second quarter of the fourteenth century. He may have been responsible for the extraordinarily delicate and visually absorbing flourishes in the St Denis Missal of *c.*1350 (plate 39).

36 Penwork flourishing, from a commentary on the Gospels. Italy (?Bologna), *c.*1200.

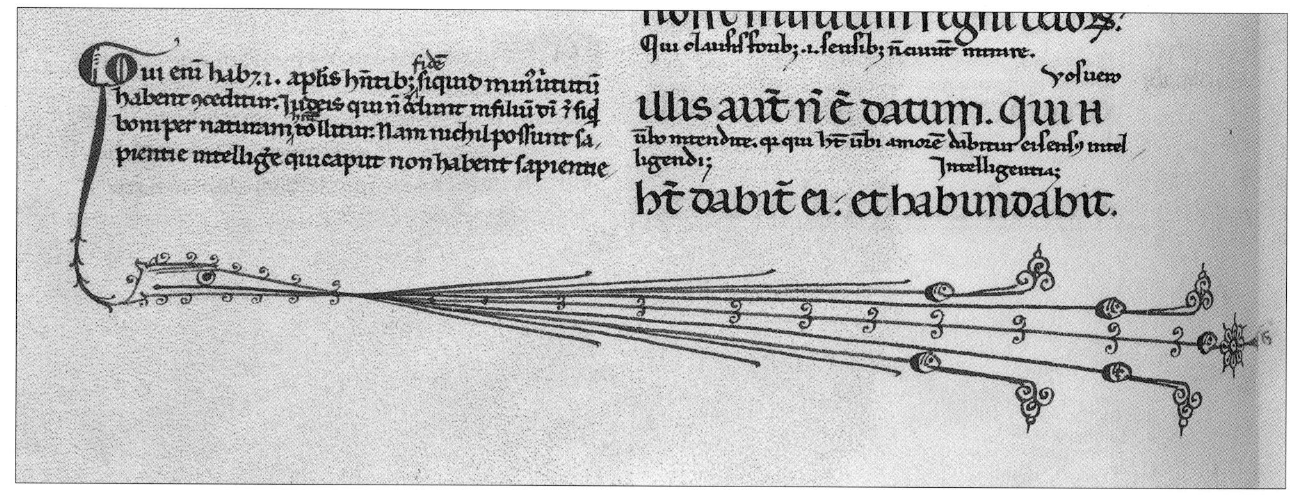

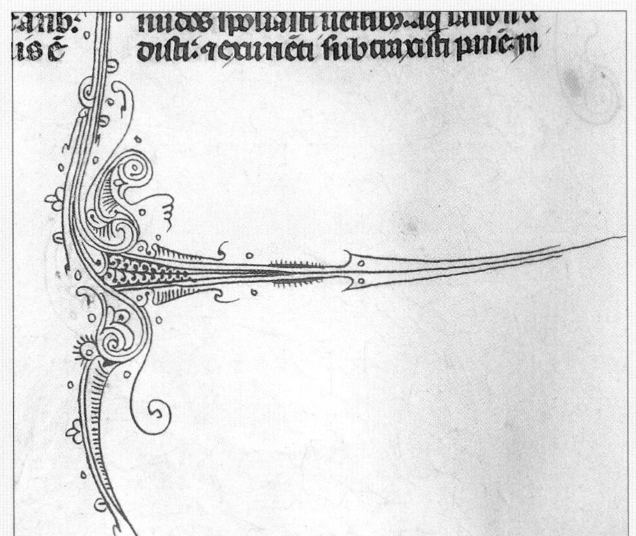

37 (above) Penwork flourishing, from a Bible. Northern Italy, *c.*1275–1300.

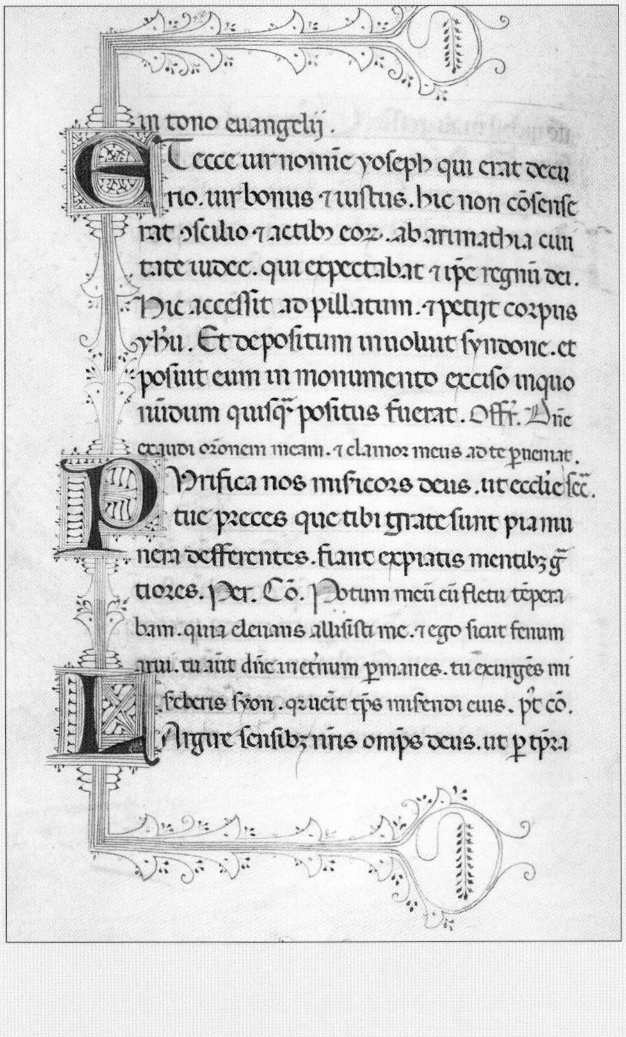

39 (right) Penwork flourishing, from the St Denis Missal. France (Paris), *c.*1350.

38 (below) Penwork flourishing, from a Missal. Italy (?Milan), *c.*1390–1400.

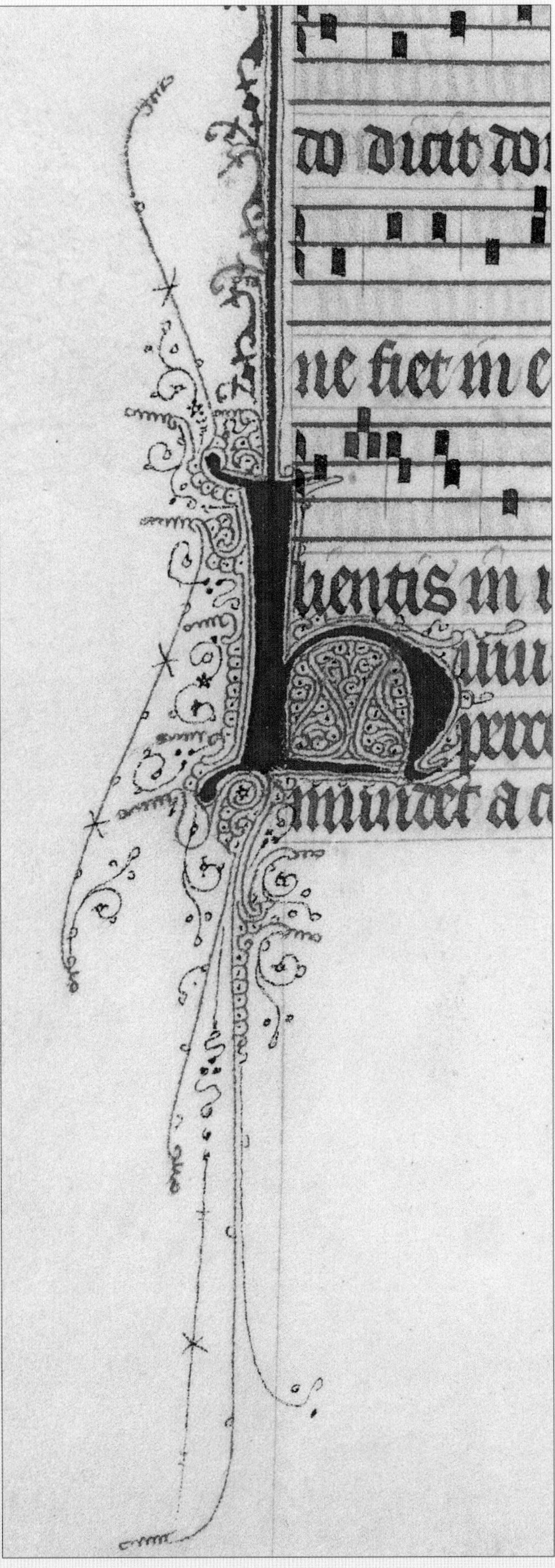

Incipiūt ep̄le. et
pphetie totius āni.
Dnīca pa de adue
tu. ep̄la. ad romnos
FRes:
Scien
tes qa
hora ē
iam nos de
sompno sur
gere. Nunc
autem ppior
est nrā salus:
qm cum cre
didimus.
Nox pcessit:
dies autem
appinquit.
Abiciamus
ergo opa te
nebrarum: 7

induamur arma lu
cis: sicut in die ho
neste ambulemus.
Non in comessatio
nibus et ebrietatibus. nō
in cubilibus et impu
dicicijs: non in cō
tentiōe et emulatiōe.
Set induimini do
minum ihm xpm.
Dnīca ij. d aduen
FRes: tu ad rom
quecūq enī
scripta sunt ad
nrām doctrinam
scripta sunt: ut per
paciam et consolatōem
scripturarum spem
habeamus. Deus
autē paciē et solatij
det nobis id ipm

5

Borders and Frames

Initials in the thirteenth century and before had antennae that reached like limbs into the margins, and these might be put on grounds bounded by cusped edges where grotesques frolicked (plate 41). Occasionally these antennae reach around the written text like a frame, as in a fourteenth-century manuscript from Umbria, which is typical of much work from northern Italy that regarded Bologna as a centre (plate 40).

By this time, illuminators in Paris had devised frames based on 'ivy-leaf' initial designs. These frames consisted of thin bands of alternate red and blue that reached around the inner and outer margins and across the bottom of the page; sprays of ivy-leaf filled margins and the tops and bottoms of the page (the lower margin or '*bas-de-page*' often being the site of images). Elongated dragons regularly formed part of this decor (plate 43). A variation of this scheme occurs in a slightly later manuscript, a biblical commentary by Nicholas de Lyra (plate 44). A cheaper solution, abundantly used from the late fourteenth century, involved a simple undulating ink line as a stem – 'string foliage' – from which issued trefoil leaves, small flowers and berries often interspersed with small spots of burnished gold to fill the margin (plate 45). This enjoyed a long future as a means of filling borders; by the mid-fifteenth century it might be used in conjunction with sprays of acanthus or flowers (the example shown here has speedwell and campion) and a U-shaped band of ornament that separates it from miniature and text (plate 46).

The use of fleshy acanthus leaves in contrasting colours as a decorative device for borders appears in the Paris book trade shortly after 1400 (plate 47), possibly

40 (left) Border ornament from an Epistle Book. Italy (Umbria), early 14th century.

41 (right) Border ornament from a Book of Hours made for use in Rheims. France (?Rheims), c.1300.

imported by an Italian illuminator (there are documentary references to contacts between Italian and Parisian illuminators at this time). Certainly, bulbous acanthus in which small figures are nested were used for marginal ornament in Italian manuscripts from at least the early fifteenth century (plate 48). In church books, this acanthus ornament was preferred to more modern Renaissance styles for most of the century (plate 50). The style associated with Ferrara but used elsewhere, consisting of a trellis of tight spirals of gold surrounded by sparsely scattered flowers or leaves, appears as a modernized version of this acanthus decoration (plate 49), quite different from the 'string foliage' mentioned above.

A border design based on multicoloured acanthus, in which the top of the leaf is blue (or another colour) and the underside brushed gold, became standard in fifteenth-century France, southern Low Countries and surrounding areas, such leaves often being interspersed with string foliage. The example shown here has the arms of Cardinal Jean Rolin, who died in 1483 (plate 51), and can be contrasted with a similar design bearing the arms of Ferry de Clugny, carried when he was Bishop of Tournai in 1473/80 (plate 52). This was developed into compartment borders, where areas of blue and brushed gold acanthus on parchment grounds were interspersed with compartments of brushed gold on which were painted semi-naturalistic flowers, fruit and berries (plate 53). The neat spirals of white acanthus tinged with grey on gold grounds that appear from mid-century have their own history (plate 54). A simplified version of this was used for printed Books of Hours, where rapidity of production was paramount.

By the fifteenth century, regional, not to say national, traditions of marginal ornament were embedded in the book trade. Distinctively English are the small acanthus leaves and flowers linked to sprays of feathered penwork stems, with a distinctive palette of lime green, blue with heavy shading in white, and pink, seen in a psalter of *c.*1430 (plate 55). In this case, the device of making up a thick band in the margin containing roundels with faces or ornament is again specifically English.

German manuscripts often contain marginal ornament with trailing stems issuing from initials that have square frames with pronounced moulding (like picture frames). The stems bear cornflowers, colombines and other

42 Border frame, from the St Denis Missal. France (Paris), *c.*1350.

flowers, in particular a leafy flower with petals radiating from a conical head (plate 56). Characteristic of Dutch manuscripts is marginal ornament with initials in coloured inks. Different patterns were favoured in different places: the version in the V&A collection is an example of the 'aubergine' category (plate 57).

Distinctive forms of ornament were developed in Italy at the end of the fifteenth century. Classical motifs copied from Roman remains include designs based on tall candelabra with vases, griffins and armour, which were suitable for the margins of books (plates 58 and 59). Such ornament was sometimes combined with acanthus scrolls (plate 60). In Florence a decorative style associated with famous miniature painters such as Attavante, but also associated with other artists, involved gold acanthus which looks more like beaten metal than anything organic, displayed in symmetrical patterns set against a rich ground of blue or red. In this scheme, multicoloured foliage was set against a gold ground, with rich areas of red, blue and a distinctive olive green. Such devices as cameo busts, roundels with portraits or devices were inserted in margins and at the top and bottom of pages (plate 61). Engraved versions of this ornamental vocabulary began to appear from the late fifteenth century – Birago's engravings of vases, acanthus, armour and putti, perhaps of *c.*1505, were evidently suitable for marginal ornament and matched his work as an illuminator. But engraved versions should be seen as perfected versions of designs that were current in the book trade (and in other trades) rather than as themselves leading a current of design. Variations of elements found in engravings appear in many manuscripts. Along with antique elements (reproductions of cameos, medals, portrait busts) in the repertory, enthusiasts of the new classicizing styles enjoyed more direct reference to archaeological research into classical remains, with reproduction of full architectural frames (plate 62), candelabra and vases, as seen in the Missal for Cardinal Giulio de' Medici illuminated by Matteo da Milano in the early sixteenth century (plate 63).

A distinctive form of ornament, developed in the southern Low Countries from just before 1480 until the mid-sixteenth century, set a standard for a kind of ornament that had an even longer life. This was the 'Ghent–Bruges' style, in which realistic flowers, fruits, insects and birds were painted in *trompe-l'oeil* on gold grounds. Simulated objects sometimes lie on the surface of the page, disregarding the layout (plate 64). In some cases, traditional grotesques and jocular scenes are integrated into the scheme, but the major impact was doubtless intended to be the hyperreal quality of the flowers and other elements (plate 65). Some people have seen symbolic meanings in these flowers, although they do not appear to have the active symbolic role of such flowers as the lily in the Annunciation or the flowers and fruit depicted with the Virgin and Child in fifteenth-century Flemish painting. It is known that in some regions cut flowers were scattered on the altar, just as on the dining table at feasts. A seventeenth-century source mentions the custom at funerals of throwing cut flowers into the grave before it was filled with earth. These associations may be prove more relevant than the discussion of allegorical symbolism about the transience of human life which surrounds some of the flower still-life paintings so popular from the early seventeenth century.

Thus far, we have considered what is conventionally termed 'secondary ornament' in manuscripts – in fact the kind of ornament that the Museum set out to collect for students and artisans in the 1850s. Archival and literary sources show that ornament constituted a discrete element in the making up of a complete illuminated page. There were illuminators who specialized in one or other aspect of this ornament. In a much-quoted passage, the author Christine de Pisan, who took to writing in the years around 1400 to support her family, referred to an illuminator named Anastasia, famous for her '*vignettes d'enluminures en livres*' or borders (until the eighteenth century 'vignette' or 'vinet' meant border, and not an ornamental drawing or picture) as well as '*champaignes d'istoires*', or landscape backgrounds for miniatures. We have already seen that André le Musnier (see p. 11) had

43 Border frame with dragon ornament, from the St Denis Missal. France (Paris), *c.*1350.

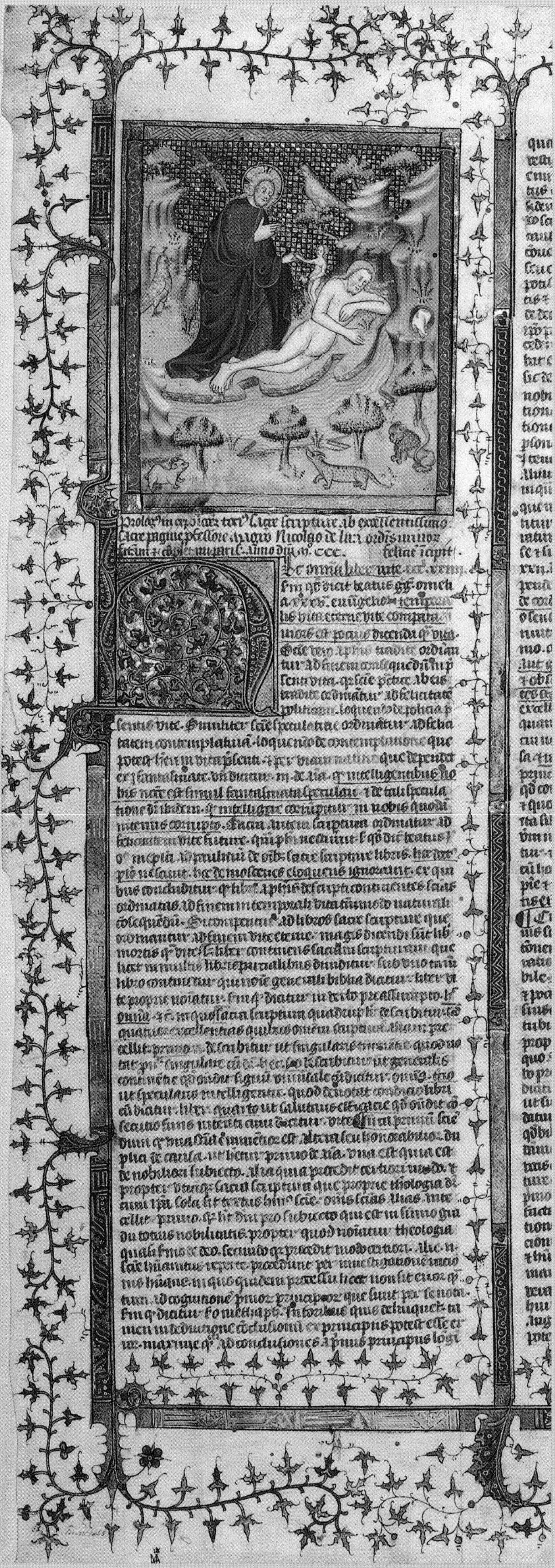

44 (opposite, left) Border ornament, from a copy of Nicholas de Lyra's commentary on the Scriptures. France (Paris), late 14th century.

45 (opposite, right) 'String foliage' border ornament, from a Book of Hours. France (Paris), c.1400–10.

46 (right) Border ornament, from a Book of Hours. Western France, 1430–40.

'*pourtraitures, histoires et vignettes*' as part of his stock. These may have resembled designs of a slightly earlier date, *c.*1440–50, that survive from England – 'vinets' and 'demi-vinets' for borders with associated initials, perhaps a sample or record of designs by more than one illuminator that could be shown to a prospective customer (Scott, no. 90).

Analysis of borders has shown that specialists and teams of specialists can sometimes be identified. Nearly a dozen manuscripts made in Paris around 1400, one of the them the Belles Heures made for the Duc de Berry, contain the work of a single border specialist. His (or her) work occurs next to that of some twenty other similar specialists (that he was independent is indicated by the fact that he did not regularly work with any of them). His work is associated with miniatures painted in a variety of styles by several other illuminators. Some decorative specialists, however, might have operated in teams and worked regularly with an individual illuminator or bookseller. The Master of the Bedford Missal, the most outstanding practitioner active in Paris around 1420–30, apparently employed a team of people responsible for secondary ornament; their work regularly appears together in manuscripts illuminated by this master.

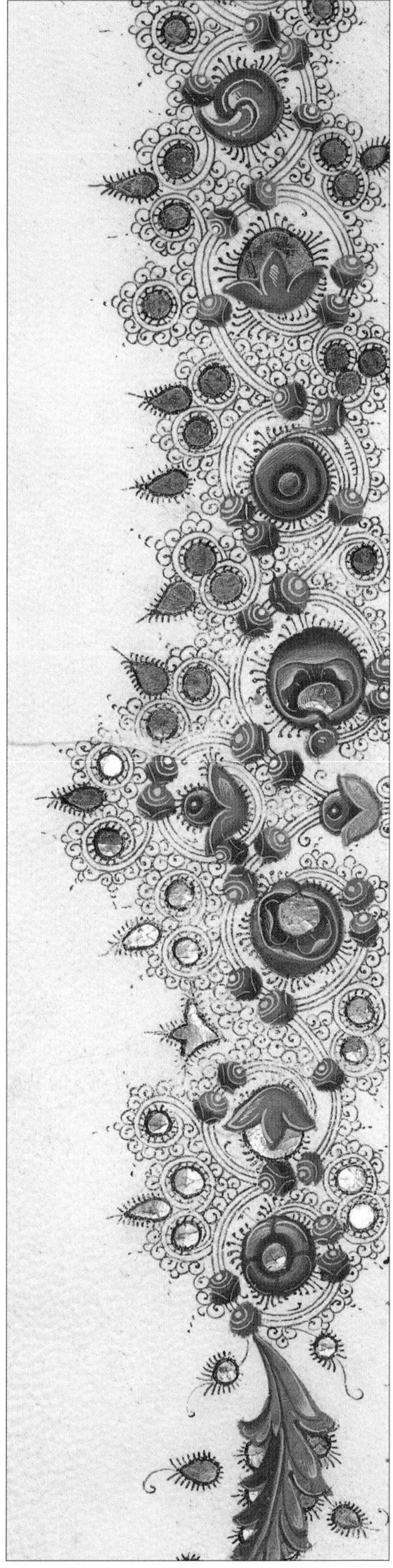

47 (opposite, left) Acanthus border ornament, from a Book of Hours. France (Paris), *c.*1400–10.

48 (opposite, centre) Acanthus border, from a Gradual. Italy (?Verona), second quarter of the 15th century.

49 (opposite, right) Border ornament. Italy, second half of the 15th century.

50 (right) Border ornament, from a choirbook. Italy, late 15th century.

51 (top) Border ornament with arms of Cardinal Jean Rolin. France, before 1483.

52 (above) Border ornament from the St Denis Missal, with arms of Ferry de Clugny as Bishop of Tournai. France, *c.*1473–80.

53 (right) Border ornament, from a Rouen Book of Hours (the 'Playfair Hours'). France (Rouen), *c.*1480.

54 (opposite left) Border ornament, from a Book of Hours. France (Rouen), *c.*1480–1500.

55 (centre left) Border ornament, from a Psalter. England (London), *c.*1430–40.

56 (left) Border from an Antiphoner. Germany, second half of the 15th century.

57 (right) Penwork border ornament, from a Book of Hours. Northern Low Countries, mid-15th century

58 (centre right) Classical border ornament, from the Bentivoglio Book of Hours. Italy, *c.*1500.

59 (far right) Classical border ornament, from Cicero's *De officiis*, written and illuminated by Bartolomeo Sanvito. Italy (Rome), 1495.

60 (below) Cut-out border ornament. Italy, second half of the 15th century.

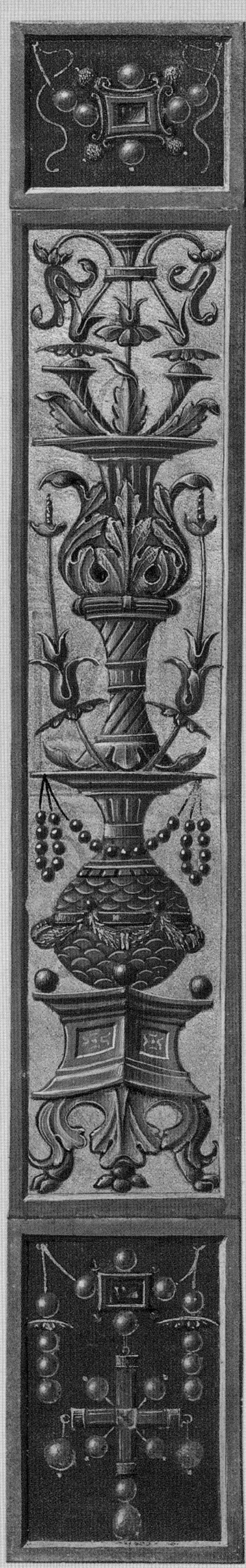

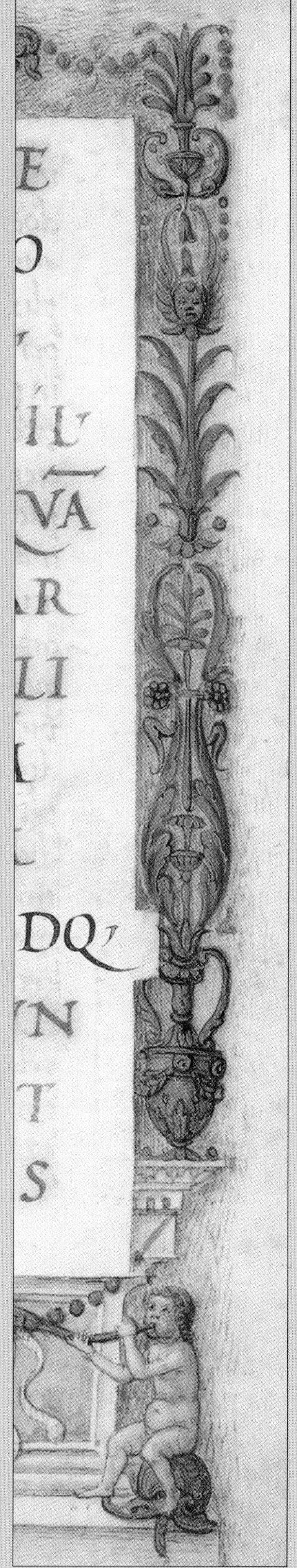

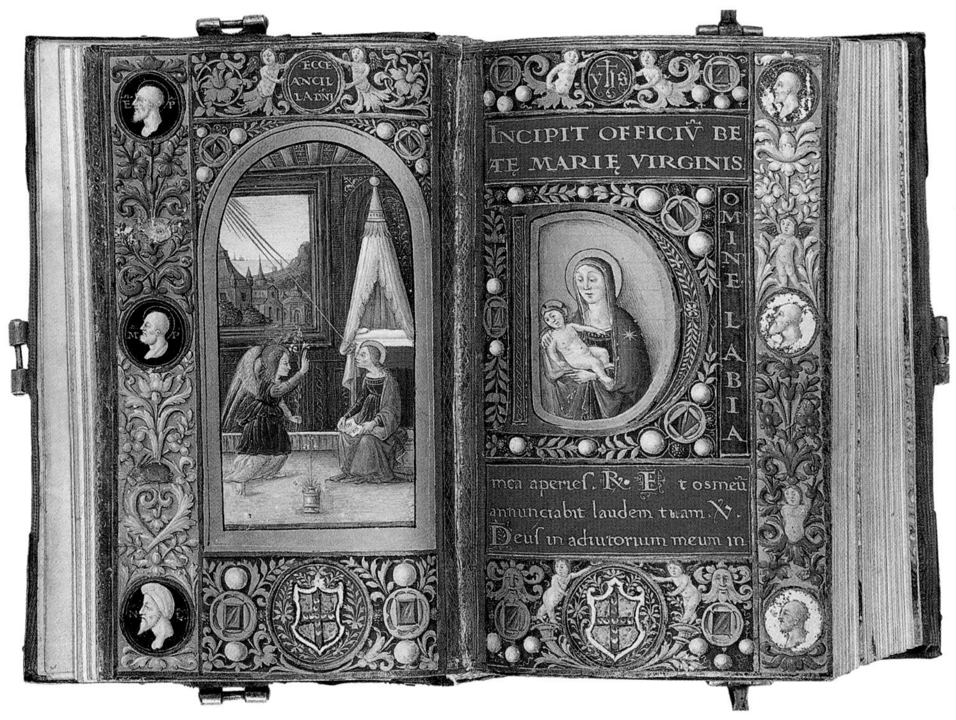
ECCE ANCILLA DNI
INCIPIT OFFICIV BEATE MARIE VIRGINIS
OMINE LABIA
mea aperies. R. Et os meu annunciabit laudem tuam. V. Deus in adiutorium meum in

VOI CHASCOL
TATE IN RIME
SPARSE IL SONO
DI QVE SOSPIRI
ONDIO NVTRI
VA IL CORE
IN SVL MIO PRIMO GIOVE
NIL ERRORE
QVANDERA IN PARTE AL
TRHVOM DA QVEL CHI SONO
DEL VARIO STILE IN CHIO
PIANGO E RAGGIONO
FRA LE VANE SPERANZE
EL VAN DOLORE
OVE SIA CHI PER PROVA
INTENDA AMORE
SPERO TROVAR PIETA NON
CHE PERDONO
MA BEN VEGGIO HOR SI CO

SANTVS IOHANNES
ZACHARIAS
SANTVS MATHEVS

61 (opposite top left) Decorated opening from a Book of Hours. Italy (Florence), *c.*1513–21.

62 (opposite left) Classical architectural frame, from the Petrarch written by Bartolomeo Sanvito. Italy (Padua), *c.*1463–64.

63 (left) Border ornament from a choirbook made for Cardinal Giulio de' Medici, illuminated by Matteo da Milano. Italy (Rome), *c.*1513–23.

64 (above) Border ornament from a 'Ghent–Bruges' Book of Hours, possibly illuminated by Simon Bening. Southern Low Countries (?Bruges), *c.*1520–30.

65 (right) Border ornament from a choirbook. Low Countries, early 16th century.

6

'SPORTS OF FANTASY': GROTESQUES

Grotesque animals and figures are no strangers to medieval art; they are much in evidence in the Gothic cathedrals that still dominate European city centres, and were much beloved of Victorian restorers. St Bernard (d.1153) famously complained that sculptural decoration in the cloister (apes, monstrous centaurs, etc.) distracted monks from their books. But such things *did* appear in books. An early thirteenth-century monk referred to the 'criminal presumption of painters that has gradually introduced these sports of fantasy'. Some clearly alluded to literary anecdotes: the use of grotesques for suits in printed fifteenth-century playing cards shows their popularity in an environment far removed from manuscripts in which they were current. From the last decades of the thirteenth century, ornament framing texts was regularly inhabited by regiments of grotesque figures, half-man and half-beast, and monsters, alongside realistically depicted animals and birds interspersed with dragons' bodies and grotesque faces. There is considerable humour in these scenes, with hares chasing dogs, for example, and battles between humanoid animals. In northern France, Flanders and England there was a particular enthusiasm for this fauna, and, in terms of painting style, elements in these burlesque scenes sometimes show a precocious naturalism.

There is occasionally a link between grotesques and text, but often there seems little more than incongruous romping. In an early fourteenth-century choirbook made for a Dominican community (and thus a very scholarly one) in the Southern Netherlands, a monkey playing a flute to catch birds graces a border next to an image of the Trinity (plate 66). If this was a satirical comment on the

chanting of the Dominicans, worse comes in a choirbook made a little later in the fourteenth century for a community of Dominican nuns in the same area, where female grotesques play musical instruments under the praying religious figures (plate 67). A marginal world of rude gesture was not inappropriate as a backdrop for sacred scenes (plate 68). There is no apparent link here between grotesque and miniature. A hybrid figure holding up a glass as if examining a urine sample before another bird-man may conceivably indicate a doctor, since the Visitation scene depicts two pregnant women (the Virgin Mary and her cousin Elizabeth), and analysis of urine was a standard means of medical diagnosis (plate 71). In the St Denis Missal, various monsters lurk in borders, but most inventive are the faces in initials that punctuate the

66 (right) Border ornament and grotesques. Southern Low Countries, *c.*1300.

67 (right and below right) Historiated initial *A* (Annunciation, with Dominican nuns), from a Dominican Gradual. Southern Low Countries, first half of the 14th century.

68 (opposite) Grotesques in a Book of Hours made for use in Rheims. France (?Rheims), *c.*1300.

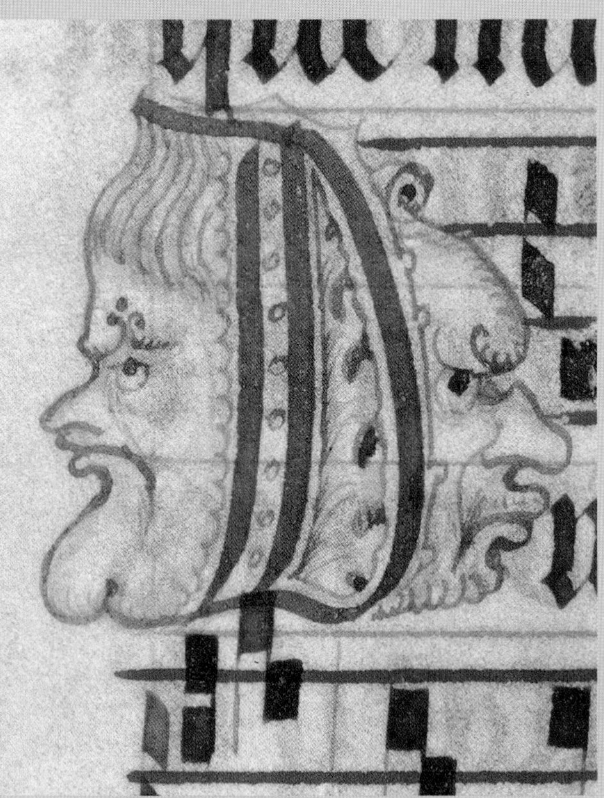

69 (left) Initials with grotesque faces from the St Denis Missal. France (Paris), *c.*1350.

70 (right) Grotesques and monsters from the borders of a Rouen Book of Hours, late 15th century.

71 (below) Grotesques in a Book of Hours made for use in Rheims. France (?Rheims), *c.*1300.

musical notation: some shout, others gape or sleep, some wear fashionable hats and dream (plate 69).

Michael Camille has suggested that this burlesque world of the margin developed in an area where the artist, rather than the text and its patron, had authority, an area where conventional hierarchies of value were subverted. The scenes can be bawdy (and obscene even by today's standards). There is, however, a consistency in the shapes and graphic ideas, which may suggest that illuminators were making variations on a theme – that there were, in fact, accepted conventions. By the fifteenth century, something like a standardized repertory appears in some environments. The borders of a Rouen Book of Hours of the 1480s include a series of dragons, birds and monkeys that looks like a set, one that was adopted for other manuscripts produced in the city (plate 70). The model book may have resembled an English manuscript of *c.*1300, now in the Pepys Library, Cambridge.

7

Miniature Painting

Apart from the production of ornament for border decoration and initials, illuminators could also provide miniatures. With increasing specialization towards the end of the Middle Ages, miniature painting became a separate activity within the book trade. Some of the first questions about the miniatures in any manuscript concern the number of individual illuminators whose work can be identified and their careers. Did they habitually work together, or can independent careers be plotted for them? Not all medieval books had miniatures, of course – most books in a princely library might, but they were possibly much rarer in books owned by working lawyers and administrators. In some books, however, miniatures were integral to their purpose, Books of Hours being the major example. (We will see examples of miniatures by illuminators from different backgrounds in Chapter 10.)

Although interest today most often focuses on images and ornament (earlier generations were more interested in texts), it was usually booksellers rather than miniature painters who dominated the book trade. Nevertheless, miniature painters were well integrated into the trade as a whole. Outstanding illuminators such as William de Brailes in thirteenth-century Oxford, Maître Honoré in Paris around 1300, and Jean Pucelle (d.1333/4) in the same city all worked with colleagues, contributing to books to which other illuminators also contributed. The Belleville Breviary of 1323–26 has a note of three illuminators who contributed. They were probably responsible for the minor decoration, and one, Mahiet, was paid by Pucelle, which indicates the latter's position. Other works by these illuminators are known; Mahiet in particular was responsible for a large number of manuscripts (referred to as 'hasty and superficial' by a modern authority) in the 1330s and 1340s. If he was the Mathew le Vavasseur who became an official *libraire* of Paris University in 1342, he was evidently commercially successful.

Pucelle is associated with a major development in artistic production. His contribution to the Jeanne d'Evreux Hours of 1325–28 shows an astonishing imitation and development of graphic ideas from Italy. There is an attempt to show spatial depth on the flat surface of the page, figures are modelled in grisaille (i.e. painting in grey), and architecture is given depth and solidity by highlighting the surfaces in direct light. Some of the compositions and conventions reflect study of Duccio's *Maestà* of 1308–11 in Siena Cathedral. Whether or not the reception of Italian art in media as varied as painting and enamelling was led by Pucelle, or whether he was an exponent of a generalized exposure to the sorts of conventions being developed in Italy, Pucelle evidently promoted a style that was taken up by a series of practitioners in the Paris book trade from the 1330s, notably the illuminator Jean le Noir (active 1335–80).

Depending on the quality of the painting, or the control of conventions to denote spatial volume and landscape, we naturally categorize manuscripts as either 'routine' or 'superior'. There can be surprising variations, however, in the quality of these aspects of work within a single manuscript. Moreover, it may not be totally satisfactory to regard routine work as a 'failed' attempt to rival the best de luxe products. This approach assumes a kind of artistic competition that may be more appropriate to

72 Prefatory full-page miniatures of St Christopher, and Christ with Mary Magdalen, from a Book of Hours made for use in Rheims. France (?Rheims), *c.*1300.

modern than to medieval conditions. Collective use of compositions and even, say, methods of building up pigment, quite apart from the ways of applying it that we call style, may represent no more than an effort to work to a common standard. Matters of finish partly depended on the amount of work a customer was prepared to finance.

The notion of the outstanding master running a workshop, training colleagues in his style, and being copied by admiring but more or less independent emulators does not fit the pattern of collaborative production. The spirit of enquiry among illuminators about pigments may well have extended to matters of style, even if not all customers put the premium on it that we do. These issues can be summed up in such questions as: is the Bedford Master the best executant of a style, or the unique creator of a style? What was the relation between people working in the same stylistic vein as the Bedford Master? For such works as the Books of Hours made for the most powerful men and women of their day, it was possibly their personal chaplains – mostly now anonymous figures – who oversaw the programme, and thus the actual writing, of text; they perhaps had the greater part in devising the programme of images.

Compositions circulated as an independent commodity – we have seen that André Le Musnier had a stock of them – and attempts to relate routine works to highly finished works are complicated by the fact that some styles acquired an autonomous life in the book trade quite independently of their original creator or creators. Around 1469–73 Maître François had the outlines of the pictures *and* the explanation of their content delivered to him for a copy of St Augustine's *City of God* that he was to illustrate – an example of an illuminator being thoroughly briefed on his work (see Avril and Reynaud, 1993, pp. 50–51). In this case the source describes Maître François' artistic skills as being superior to those of the classical Greek artist Apelles (the writer was keen to use classical epithets and vaunt his humanistic education). For unusual images, aids were particularly necessary; Jean le Begue gave an account of a programme of images for a text of Sallust in *c.*1417, and in 1539 the humanist scholar Louis Vivès was sent by Mencia de Mendosa to instruct Simon Bening on the images to be put into a Book of Hours being ordered.

73, 74 (left) Miniatures of the Sacrifice of Abraham, the Resurrection, and the Annunciation, from the St Denis Missal. France (Paris), *c.*1350.

75 (opposite) Presentation in the Temple, from a Book of Hours, Use of Le Mans. Western France. *c.*1430–40.

Some illuminators worked quite outside the commercial environment. The Limbourg brothers, members of the household of the Duc de Berry before their presumed death in 1416, developed an astonishingly avant-garde art with topographical paintings and versions of advanced Italian practice. Their work had little impact on illumination done by others. Jean Fouquet was responsible for the famous Hours of Etienne Chevalier of *c.*1452–60, and a number of its compositional ideas if not its rich Italianate ornamental vocabulary were copied by others. On the whole, however, Fouquet contributed to books made by other people, working as a painter as much as an illuminator (from *c.*1475 until his death *c.*1481 he was painter to the king). Jean Bourdichon, on the other hand, although working from 1491 as painter, decorator and illuminator at a royal castle near Tours, often used compositions that could be found elsewhere in the book trade, though their careful execution and finish surpassed most contemporary work. Some of the most inventive and original works of the fifteenth century were perhaps produced in these sheltered environments.

At less exalted levels of production, groups of people worked in a particular style, and – without constituting a workshop – may have had some kind of settled relationship. Such relationships are most apparent in the case of Paris painters such as the Boucicaut Master, originally from Bruges, whose Italianisms support his identification with Jacques Coene of Paris, an artist who worked at Milan Cathedral *c.*1410, or with his later follower, the Duke of Bedford Master. In these cases, it does not seem possible to group all works in their style as products of a workshop under the master's direction, but as part of a stylistic trend adopted by a group of illuminators – a free association rather than a hierarchical workshop – who worked in the Paris book trade.

Illuminators' skill lay not only in creating or adapting images but also in preparing colours. They used a variety of pigments, and contemporaries were probably acutely aware of the characteristics of each. Some, such as André Le Musnier, possibly dealt in pigments (see p. 11). Contracts for paintings (many survive for late medieval Italy), for example, were usually predominantly concerned with quality of pigment. Leonardo da Vinci complained around 1500 that 'the ignorant masses . . . require nothing of painting other than beauty of colour.' Pigments were made from minerals and plant extracts, and their preparation was one of the essential skills of the illuminator as it was of the painter. In 1480 the illuminator Evrard d'Espinques was working in the village of Ahun in La Marche. He had originally come from Cologne to study in Paris and had been installed by Jacques d'Armagnac, Duke of Nemours, in Ahun to work on the duke's books. In the account he made to Armagnac's successor, Pierre de Beaujeu, of work done between 1 August 1479 and 1 November 1480, he provided a long list of the pigments he had used for *hystoires*, *figures*, *lettres* and *vignectes*. Gold was used, 11 ounces of *azur*, *roze de Paris*, and so on. The term '*achampir*' was used for the provision of initials and grounds for large letters, showing that this was regarded as a specific task. The separate accounting for '*floret*' (probably flourishing) used to finish off ('*arrondir*') the '*hystoires*' again suggests an element of decoration that was regarded as an independent technique.

For the grandest manuscripts, ground lapis lazuli provided a translucent blue, but azurite (a copper ore) was more generally used. Treatment of lead provided white (carbonate of lead) and red (minium), and copper was the basis of various greens, as was terre verte. Orpiment (arsenic sulphide) provided a yellow. Vegetable-based pigments (lakes) included indigo and woad for blue, while madder and brazil wood gave reds. The medium for pigments was usually glair prepared from egg-whites. There was considerable technical advance in the production of colours during the Middle Ages, and much lively discussion of methods and technical advances. This is evident in the treatise of the 1430s by Jean Le Begue when he put in order the notes of Jehan Alcherius, an illuminator and painter who moved between Paris and northern Italy between 1382

and 1410. The celebrated manual of Cennino Cennini, *Il libro dell'arte*, written *c.*1400, similarly testifies to a lively spirit of research: while its first paragraphs relate to drawing materials, the first substantial sections discuss the preparation of pigments.

In an environment in which multicoloured images and ornament were not as omnipresent as they are today, colour was probably one of the chief qualities for which early owners prized their illuminated manuscripts. Much illumination depends on quite a limited range of pigments. A dazzling visual effect could be achieved with the bold juxtaposition of areas of plain colour, as for example in the series of prefatory full-page images of a Book of Hours made for Rheims *c.*1300: a bright orange red, a matt red, a green, blue and shades of brown (plate 72) with burnished gold as a background. Heavy black outline drawing is used for the figures, with the more delicate facial features drawn in ink, and the eyes carefully sited to show direction and contact between the actors (this is not a style in which bodies are moulded in colour in the round).

The pigments in the St Denis Missal of *c.*1350 are rather purer. The background in the miniatures for the sacrifice of Abraham and the martyrdom of St Andrew are in rich, saturated colours with highlighted patterning in brushed gold or white. The figures are carefully moulded in the round in the grisaille technique made fashionable by Pucelle. The exchange of glances between Abraham and the angel shows a definite attempt to demonstrate the nature of the angelic message, while the grimaces of St Andrew's tormentors express the evil intent of the murderers (see p.90). Christ rising from the tomb over the body of a sleeping soldier in fourteenth-century armour is a rather compressed scene in the manner of the poorer qualities of the Annunciation scene. The figures are inexpressive and the drawing weak. If the mud-green ground with small shoots is characteristic of this painter (all the images by this master in an illustrated Bible done for the French king Jean le Bon in 1349–52 have this feature), the quality of this particular work falls short of other miniatures in the manuscript and, indeed, other work attributed to him (plates 73 and 74). If it was indeed the colour that gave the images value for early readers, such weaknesses in drawing and figurative painting were perhaps allowable.

Miniatures in a Book of Hours from Angers or Rennes of *c.*1430–40 show a reliance for effect on broad areas of a single colour, though some areas are modelled with light and dark to show the pose of the body beneath. Various conventions are used to show spatial recession in buildings – unsuccessfully to modern eyes (they are less controlled than similar architectural apses associated with the best Boucicaut Master manuscripts). The features are efficiently portrayed with a minimum of strokes, and, while they show the direction of the gaze, they do not show meaningful contact between the people concerned (plate 75).

Colour and the depiction of fashionable dress appear to be the chief concerns in a miniature done in England around the same date (plate 76). The painting of the faces employs such conventions as a light line for the ridge of the nose; rosebud mouths; and beady black eyes. The expressions of David and his courtiers go some way towards expressing alarm, but the grimaces of the assailants are more cheerful than threatening.

The basic repertory of colours is similar in a Book of Hours of *c.*1500 from Paris or Rouen (plate 77). This style had a wide currency. It relied on bright, shiny surfaces; white faces for women and darker ones for men; and large areas of single colours with modelling in dark lines or brushed gold. The coloured panels in the wall and pillars reveal an economical way of suggesting new Renaissance architectural styles. Where Italianate frames are depicted, the detail is picked out in red lines; the bushes and blue distances in the scene of David in Penitence are totally

76 (opposite) Miniature of David stoned and shamed by Shimei, from a Psalter. England, *c.*1430.

77 (right) David in Penitence, from a Book of Hours. France (Rouen or Paris), *c.*1500.

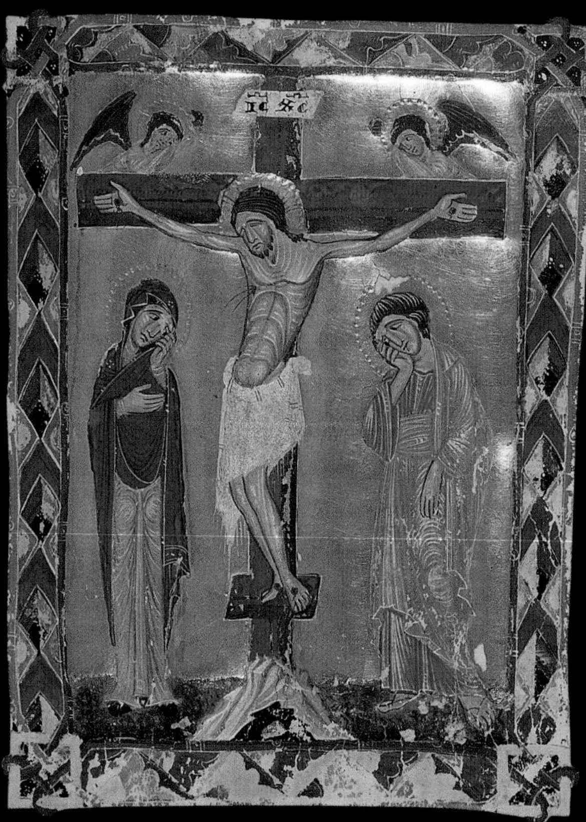

78 Crucifixion scene, from a Missal. Italy (?Veneto), 14th century.

79 (right) Historiated initial (the death of Joshua; Book of Judges), from a Bible. Northern Italy, *c.*1275–1300.

0 Beheading of St John the
Baptist, in an initial *O* from a
choirbook. Northern Italy, early
15th century.

81 Crucifixion with the Virgin Mary and John the Evangelist, in a historiated initial *I* from a choirbook. Northern Italy, early 15th century.

82 (left) Two apostles with books, in an initial *E* from a choirbook. Northern Italy, early 15th century.

83 (below) St Francis, in an initial *O* from a choirbook. Northern Italy, early 15th century.

84 (opposite) St Giustina before the Emperor Maximilian, with the signature of Girolamo da Cremona, in an initial *M* from a choirbook. Italy (?Padua), late 1460s.

formulaic as a means of showing aerial perspective and can be paralleled in hundreds of similar manuscripts.

In comparison with French and English miniatures, works from Italy can show a radically different range of colours. Early miniatures adhere to both the colour scheme and graphic conventions of icons in Byzantinizing style (plate 78). The miniatures in a late thirteenth-century Bible are characteristic of works in the area that took its lead from Bologna in the use of a rich blue, a grey or slate blue, contrasted with bright orange and ochre (plate 79).

In Italy, illuminated choirbooks and liturgical manuscripts contain the work of large numbers of miniature painters. Choirbooks in particular were produced in sets of many volumes (often more than thirty). When in 1457 Siena Cathedral decided to replace a thirteenth-century set, the work lasted for more than fifty years. Cathedral archives record the names of some of the most outstanding illuminators of Italy who came from all parts to undertake the work. From the early nineteenth century onwards, such choirbooks provided an easy source of images that connoisseurs eagerly sought to add to their collections of paintings. Their custodians had little notion of their potential financial or artistic worth, and perhaps reflected that such books could continue to function without their initials.

A group of cuttings reflects northern Italian work of the first part of the fifteenth century. Giovanni dei Grassi was the outstanding personality in Milanese illumination around 1400, and exemplified the luxurious International Gothic style associated with the area. The work attributed to Tomasino da Vimercate, however, was perhaps more representative (plate 80). The miniature showing the Beheading of St John attributed to this illuminator testifies to a colourful style that would look old-fashioned once Belbello da Pavia and his like emerged. This conservatism was maintained by a miniature painter known as the Master of the Vitae Imperatorum (after a manuscript made for Filippo Maria Visconti, Duke of Milan, in 1431). It represents a specifically Lombard style with bright colours, dramatic close-up figures, strong black outlines that enclose areas of modulated colour, drapery with long, straight folds, and expressive faces (plate 81). This master illuminated classical texts for the Visconti court as well as religious manuscripts. His work reflects a pictorial tradition that flourished in ducal Milan, a place that absorbed Renaissance styles from Tuscany and the Veneto only later in the century; the ornament in some of his major works betrays imitation of French illumination. From the same environment are cuttings by an illuminator known as the Olivetan Master (two apostles on a vermiculated blue ground; plate 82), and by the Master of the Franciscan Breviary, in which the face and drapery of St Francis displaying his stigmata are treated in a more sophisticated fashion (plate 83).

IERONIMUS

85 Two Benedictine bishops, with the signature of Bartolomeo de' Rigossi da Gallarate, in an initial *M* from a choirbook. Northern Italy, third quarter of the 15th century.

86 David harping, by Girolamo dai Libri, in an initial *B* from a choirbook. Italy (Verona), *c.*1495.

SIMO·BINNIK·ALEXADRI·F·
SEIPSV·PIGEBAT·ANO·ÆTATIS 75

We are thrown into a different world with a miniature of Santa Giustina disputing with grammarians and rhetoricians before the Emperor Maximilian. This is signed by the illuminator, Girolamo da Cremona ('*Ieronimus f[ecit]*') at the base of the fluted column (plate 84). The carefully painted receding pillars, the coffered ceiling, the contrapposto pose of the green figure, and the acanthus scrolls of the letter shape all denote familiarity with the conventions of the best contemporary painting. Girolamo led a peripatetic career: he worked in Modena on the famous Bible of Borso d'Este in Ferrara before moving to Mantua. This miniature was probably executed in Padua, after which he contributed to the celebrated *corali* in Siena. From the mid-1470s he worked in Venice illustrating printed books. Another signed initial of the 1470s is by one Bartolomeo de' Rigossi da Gallarate (plate 85), a name that links him with the area around Milan. This appears unadventurous compared Girolamo's work, but the figures of two Benedictine bishops, one of them perhaps Ambrose of Milan, have the monumental presence that was required of an initial in a choirbook, even if the recession of the beams on top of the architectural niche is not properly worked out.

Illumination continued to be a prized art well in to the sixteenth century. Vasari, writing in the second half of the century, singled out the work of Girolamo dai Libri, who was both a painter and illuminator. The initial in the Museum by this illuminator was perhaps done in Girolamo's native Verona, just before 1500 (plate 86). Vasari praised the work of his contemporary, the illuminator Giulio Clovio (1498–1578), but he does not include other work from the period represented by miniatures in the V&A (plate 87) in a High Renaissance painterly style.

Signed miniatures were a rarity, even in Italy. By the time that Vasari was praising Clovio as the Michelangelo of illumination, it had become the work of specialists rather than a 'trade' that underpinned production. The latest group of miniature painters that can be called a 'school' were the so-called 'Ghent–Bruges' school in Flanders. Italian businessmen, diplomats and churchmen commissioned works from them in the late fifteenth century, and Vasari had a dim notion of the names of individual illuminators. He mentioned members of the Horenbout family and Simon Bening, and was impressed by the service of such people for the English monarchs Henry VIII and Elizabeth I. It may have been his links with royal and noble clients that encouraged Simon Bening to execute a self-portrait of himself (plate 88), a kind of equivalent of Vespasiano da Bisticci's account of his trade and customers over half a century earlier (see p. 11). In the sixteenth century the production of miniatures increasingly survived only as a niche within the de luxe trade.

87 (right)The Finding of The Cross and border ornament, from a choirbook. Italy, late 16th century.

88 (opposite) Self-portrait by the illuminator Simon Bening. Southern Low Countries (Bruges), *c.*1550–60.

8

WORKING METHODS

Medieval manuscripts rarely provide many obvious clues as to how they were made, or the relationships between the people who made them. Many have been trimmed to fit modern bindings and had fly-leaves removed, so that marks that would tell us about the production process have been removed. Rebinding has been the bane of research in this field – one can sympathize with William Morris's anguish at what 'the fury of the binders knife' has destroyed. The basic unit of production was the individual bifolium; each bifolium, or each gathering of bifolia, could be worked on by different people. A thirteenth-century missal in the V&A that was unbound in the nineteenth century allows us to see how the bifolia were fitted together to make a quire; the initials in each quire were done by different individuals or teams (plate 89). One or two manuscripts from *c.*1400 show that the writing could be done on a large sheet (an imposed sheet) ruled for two bifolia (i.e. with all two or four rectos written before turning over the uncut parchment sheet and writing the versos in such a way that when folded and cut, the text would run on), much as printing is done today. The use of small numbers and of quire catchwords can sometimes be seen, which shows how the scribe and illuminator kept bifolia in order for passing on to other craftsmen.

The basic page design took place at the writing stage, since it was here that spaces were left for miniatures, initials and ornament. A missal written perhaps in the Veneto *c.*1300 contains spaces left by the scribe for illuminated initials. Those decorated with penwork and flourishing have been completed as part of a separate scheme of work (plate 90). Within this same manuscript, another kind of initial was left incomplete. We can see here that the shape of the initial was drawn with red ink of a different kind from that used elsewhere in the book. The parts destined for gold leaf were prepared with a layer of white bole; the gold leaf was applied as the first step; and the red ground of the letter-shape and any major decorative feature was then applied (plate 91). What these initials lack is the final finishing in which further pigment would be applied and the edges of the gold and colours tidied up.

Where parts of a manuscript remain unfinished, it can be possible to argue that different sets of people played different roles in making the book. It is easy to explain why some manuscripts stayed unfinished: high-quality work required investment over a long period. This was the case, for example, with the marvellous Book of Hours from Provence of *c.*1440–50 in the Pierpont Morgan Library, illuminated by Barthélemy d'Eyck and others. What lay behind the unfinished state of the Hours owned by 'Harreteau' (now in the V&A), perhaps made in the Tours area in the 1490s, is not known. Here some elements are complete and others not. A miniature of St Mark on the verso of folio 16 shows that a high level of finish was being aimed at. The face is built up with carefully stippled pigments against a ground of reflective grey (plate 92). The other miniatures, however, are unfinished. The Annunciation (plate 93) has no more than the initial washes to denote the areas of figures and grounds (the pencil drawing on the Virgin's face reveals a drawing school convention of parallel lines to situate the nose centrally). The half-page miniatures have only some finished elements: the figures are mostly in the state of

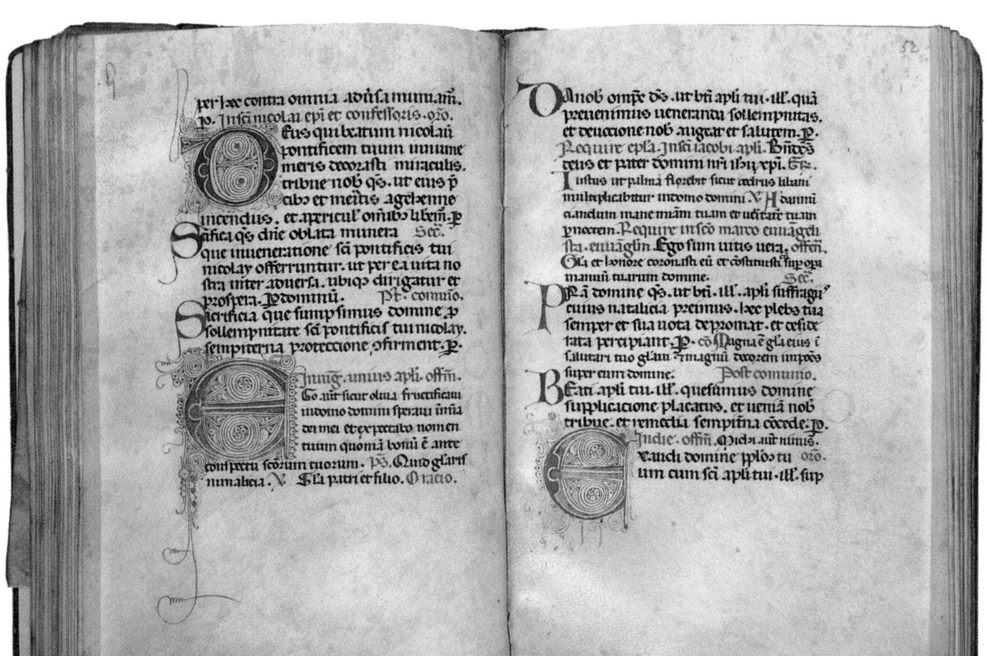

89 (above) Gathering (also called a quire) of bifolia from a monastic Missal. Southern France, 13th century.

90 (left) Penwork initials in a Missal. Italy (?Veneto), 14th century.

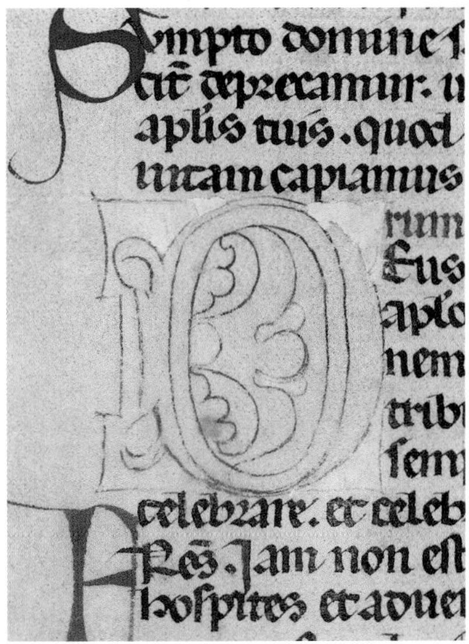

91 (above) Unfinished initials drawn in red ink, prepared with bole, with gold and coloured grounds added, in a Missal. Italy (?Veneto), 14th century.

92 (below) St Mark, from a Book of Hours (the 'Harreteau Hours'). France (?western or northern), c.1490–1500.

washes, ready to receive the next layer of pigment to build up detail of clothes and faces. At the same time, the borders around these miniatures are actually complete.

A significant feature of the three full-page miniatures is that they include elements that appear fully finished alongside others that are left untouched. The distant town behind the castle walls in the scene of David watching Bathsheba is complete, but Bathsheba herself has only the gold of her skirt brushed in (plate 94). In the scene of the horsemen meeting the death figures (an ancient story in which the young and wealthy are reminded of their mortality), the townscape and landscape are complete, but the horsemen are barely touched. Moreover, the drawing in this miniature is much more complicated than is needed to guide the person who would apply the pigment washes (plate 95). It would seem, therefore, that drawings were done by artists who were not working in conjunction with the colourists whose job was to put in the initial washes – their skill was drawing, and they did more than provide an outline. Whether they also drew the marginal ornament to guide the illuminators cannot be deduced, but the fact that the borders in this manuscript are finished suggests that they formed part of a separate campaign.

Drawing was a evidently a distinct skill in its own right. Interestingly, in German-speaking lands, drawing – sometimes with coloured washes – was systematically used to illustrate books. It formed the basis, for example, of the books, including vernacular texts and illustrated Bibles in German, issued by the schoolmaster and bookdealer Diebold Laubers in Hagenau between at least 1425 and 1467 (three of his sales lists are known). This sort of production, with freely invented illustrative cycles drawn in paper volumes, contrasts with more westerly regions, where illumination with colours and gold, or gold substitutes, on parchment was the standard of commercial book production.

Returning to the Harreteau Hours, it seems that the artists who put in the washes for the half-page miniatures over the drawn images were not themselves draughtsmen – there is an attempt to doodle faces to provide the light and dark of cheek and eye-socket but no evidence of the ability to carry this out (plate 96). Whether or not the people or teams involved habitually worked together in

93 (top left) Annunciation (unfinished) from the 'Harreteau Hours'. France (?western or northern), *c*.1490–1500.

94 (top right) David and Bathsheba (unfinished), from the 'Harreteau Hours'. France (?western or northern), *c*.1490–1500.

95 (bottom left) Horsemen meeting death figures (unfinished), from the 'Harreteau Hours'. France (?western or northern), *c*.1490–1500.

96 (bottom right) Annunciation to the Shepherds (unfinished), from the 'Harreteau Hours'. France (?western or northern), *c*.1490–1500.

some kind of organized workshop arrangement cannot be known – scholars today are less ready to assume that they were systematically linked in this way.

The problems posed by the Harreteau manuscript are similar to those identified by Kathleen Scott in relation to six manuscripts decorated in London in around 1465. She defines these as issuing from a shop in which two border illuminators operated; the manuscripts also contained the work of four other miniature painters. Did each have their own shop, their own independent career, or did they come together on an *ad hoc* basis for these six commissions?

If we think in terms of 'campaigns', with each level, from drawing to final finishing, done by different people

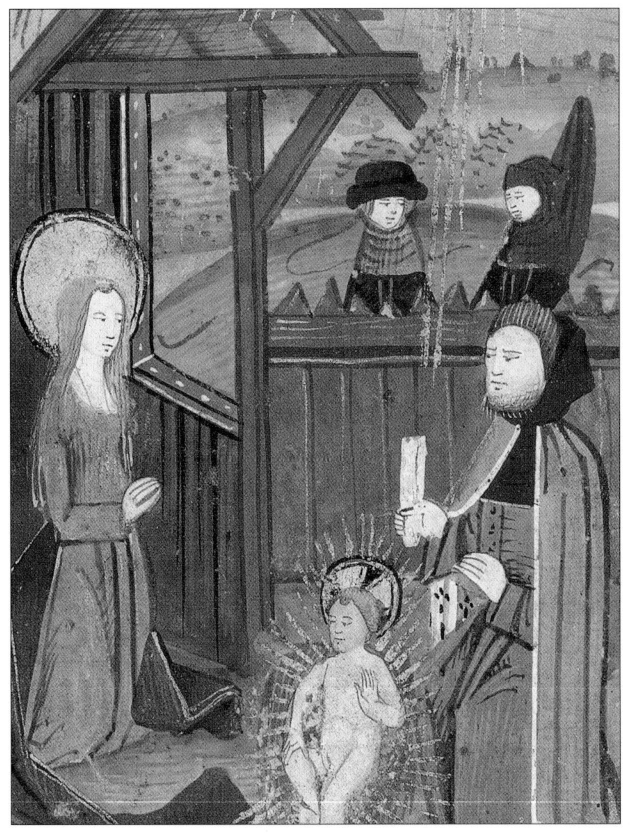

or at different times, it explains mistakes that can be observed in some manuscripts. In a Book of Hours made in Bruges for the English market in the third quarter of the fifteenth century, the Nativity scene includes farm workers who look in at the Holy Family. One has a cloak flowing vertically upwards in the wind. Since a common version of this composition contains angels rather than farm workers, it seems probable that the draughtsman drew angels but that the colourist turned these into farm workers, with an angel's wing becoming a strange erect cloak (plate 97). There are similar examples of such misunderstandings, in which either the model sketched in or the written instructions to the illuminator in the margin are misinterpreted, implying lack of direct contact between the person giving the instruction and the person executing it.

What were the sources of the images used for manuscripts such as this? Although model books maintained by illuminators and workshops do survive, there are so few that their generalized existence remains a hypothesis. The shared use of compositions by groups of illuminators supports this theory, unless their training involved procedures that encouraged certain conventions – once you had sketched out your hundredth Annunciation scene or painted your hundredth face, you

97 (above left) Nativity scene from a Book of Hours (the 'Zouche Hours') made for the English market. Southern Low Countries (?Bruges), *c.*1470–80.

98 (left) Adoration of the Magi, from a Book of Hours (the 'Playfair Hours'). France (Rouen), *c.*1480.

99 (right) Adoration of the Magi, from a Book of Hours. France (Rouen), *c.*1480.

100 (left) Moses and the burning bush, from the blockbook *Biblia pauperum*. Germany, 1460s.

101 (right) Moses and the burning bush, from a Book of Hours (the 'Playfair Hours'). France (Rouen), *c*.1480.

102 (left) Sacrifice of Abraham, from the blockbook *Biblia pauperum*. Germany, 1460s.

103 (right) The sacrifice of Abraham, from a Book of Hours (the 'Playfair Hours'). France (Rouen), *c*.1480.

could probably do them in a certain manner without undue thought. Some environments are associated with highly standardized production, for instance Rouen in the last third of the fifteenth century. In terms of compositions, there is a close similarity between, for example, the Adoration of the Magi in the Playfair Hours of the 1480s and another Rouen book of a similar date (plates 98 and 99), both of them similar to those used by the rather earlier – and much better – illuminator formerly known as the Master of the Geneva Latini and recently dubbed the Master of the Echevins of Rouen. This scene was a common one, and it is similar to that used in the *Biblia pauperum*, the blockbook (so-called since each page is printed from a single woodcut) of *c*.1460 with scenes of the biblical story that was widely distributed throughout Europe. Details in the Playfair Hours are in fact very similar to some scenes in the *Biblia pauperum* – Moses and the Burning Bush or Abraham's

104 (above) Border ornament and deer. Germany, second half of the 15th century.

105 (right) Engraved playing card with deer. Germany, mid-15th century (before 1446).

sacrifice of Isaac – which makes it conceivable that some kind of copying had taken place (plates 100, 101, 102 and 103). Details of compositions frequently circulated as well as the compositions themselves, perhaps reflecting the selective copying by illuminators of scenes as they built up their own repertories. Playing cards provided one source of imagery; these were printed (as engravings or woodcuts), and suits might be birds, beasts or deer. A German initial of the second half of the fifteenth century copies a deer from the 'Three of Deer' card of one such suit (plates 104 and 105).

New ways were found from the 1430s and 1440s to mass produce images through woodcuts and prints. The images circulated in this way, which were often of very traditional compositions, were used selectively in the book trade. Engravings such as those of Martin Schongauer were widely used as a source for paintings, sculptural friezes and even illuminated miniatures. There are a few groups of related manuscripts, attributed to notional workshops, that apparently relied on specific sets of prints for their images. In general, however, the book trade already had a sufficient store of compositions amassed by traditional means, whether in model books or ingrained in working practices, to disregard them. Printed Books of Hours containing illustrations were available from the mid-1480s, but it was not until after 1500 that the manuscript variety gave way to the new technology. By this time artists who might have been illuminators were either providing designs for woodcuts and engravings needed by the new technology of print or finding other ways of supplying coloured images cheaply to meet the demands of the new industry.

9

MASS-PRODUCED MEDIEVAL BOOKS

It has been said that the printing of Bibles underpinned the Victorian book trade. In fact, at almost every period, some particular kind of book becomes a token of its age with a special importance for the economics of the book trade. For example, after the mid-twelfth century, when Paris became a centre for study of the Scriptures, the city also became a centre for the production of glossed Bibles (the canons of St Victor and others made arrangements for their production by scribes from various backgrounds). Another example concerns French literary texts from the fourteenth century, which Richard and Mary Rouse have identified as of special importance for Paris book-makers. The same can be said of Books of Hours from a slightly later date. This chapter examines the success of medieval book-makers in responding to the demands of their age.

Up to the twelfth century, monasteries were the major European centres of economic, government and cultural activities. The thirteenth century saw the development of great bureaucracies to control a growing population, much of it now living in towns and cities. The church sought to ensure that people respected the disciplines of Christian life; work in the community, rather than in isolated monasteries, was needed. Orders such as the Franciscans and Dominicans were not ensconced in monasteries but integrated into secular life. Their members, the friars, eschewed wealth (Franciscans were initially not allowed to own property) and undertook extensive pastoral duties, especially preaching. For this they needed the complete text of the Bible in a portable format, as well as new devices to enable easy access to distinct parts of the text, namely indexes of all kinds.

Pocket Bibles were developed in Paris (where book-makers had had to supply other texts for academic study in compact formats in the years around 1200). These books were written on wafer-thin parchment, of a kind once called 'uterine' – it was perhaps made from the skins of still-born cattle (a stationer in Florence in 1426 had skins of *cavrecti non nati* – i.e. unborn baby goats, *capretti* in Italian – listed among his stock). However, manuscripts of this kind survive in such quantities that some way of splitting parchment may also have been used. Pocket Bibles were made easily usable by indexes and foliation, and by judicious illumination (capitals in red and blue, running titles, chapter numbers).

The model was developed in Paris and soon imitated, so that it is often difficult to tell whether a particular manuscript was done in Paris, Oxford or elsewhere. The more luxurious sort had initials illuminated with gold and figurative scenes. A pocket Bible in the V&A (plate 106) dating from the second half of the thirteenth century has illumination that seems Italian, done in imitation of the Parisian model. The margins in this manuscript were left wide and bare in many examples. Such margins were used by owners to compile their own commentaries and add notes, often linked to the text or to a specific theme by an indexing symbol. Attentive reading and absorption of the text is indicated by the pointing hand and the bishop's head, a rather crude indexing device. Annotations in books of this kind show that many were being used in the later Middle Ages and beyond. It has been argued that thirteenth-century production was so substantial that the market for such works was satisfied until small printed Bibles appeared in the sixteenth century.

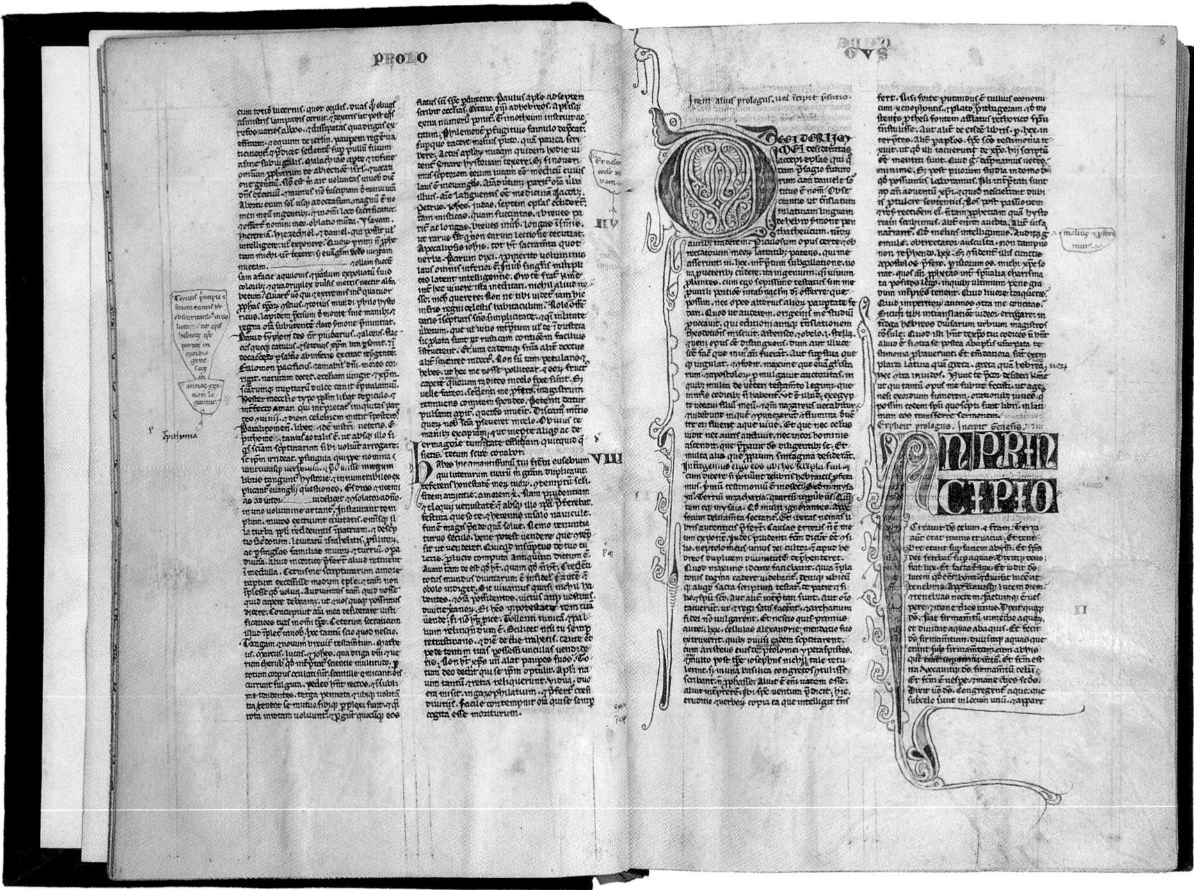

Books of Hours are another example of mass-produced manuscripts. Part of their interest lies in the solutions devised for maximizing production – they are a wonderful source for discovering how manufacture and marketing worked in the late medieval book trade. The V&A has a Book of Hours made in Bruges *c.*1440–50 with some remarkable indications of how it was produced. The manuscript was evidently intended for the English market (it followed the Use of Sarum – the form of devotions prescribed for Salisbury and the archdiocese of Canterbury) (plates 107 and 108). The miniatures in this manuscript are all on single leaves, the pigment on them contrasting with that used elsewhere in the book (the blues are quite different, as are the reds, oranges and light greens). The miniatures are in the so-called 'Masters of Otto of Moerdrecht' style (a group of miniaturists named after a manuscript owned by a canon of Utrecht that was given to the Carthusian monastery of Nieuwlicht in 1424). It is characterized by slim, swaying, doll-like figures with contrasting areas of crude colour and burnished gold for landscape background.

These leaves bear a little stamp, almost invisible, in the bottom right-hand corner, a gothic *b* reserved in red. James Farquhar identified several manuscripts containing miniatures stamped in this way, and related them to legislation by the Bruges authorities to control the importing of single-leaf images for books. The legislation implies a settled relationship within Bruges between the sellers of books, book-makers and illuminators. The importing of miniatures to be inserted into books undermined this relationship, since they could undercut the price of the locally produced article (those from Utrecht were singled out for special mention). Such imported miniatures were traded between book-makers as well as being bought for immediate insertion by book-makers into their own books. The importing of whole books containing images had been agreed by legislation of 1403. In 1426 it was declared that only miniatures

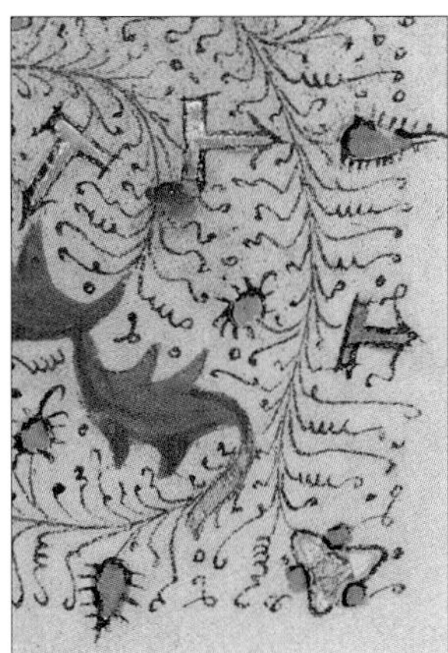

106 (opposite) Single volume 'pocket' Bible. Italy, second half of the 13th century.

107 (right) Christ carrying the cross from a Book of Hours. Southern Low Countries (Bruges), c.1440–50.

108 (above) Border ornament from a Book of Hours. Southern Low Countries (Bruges), c.1440-50.

produced within the city could be used, and that these could not be re-sold. Every person making such images – and it is clear that single-leaf miniatures such as those in the V&A Book of Hours with illuminators' stamps were involved – had to register their sign with the guild that policed the craft, and pay a charge of 40 Paris shillings. As in many other cities, it became the rule in Bruges that only those with the status of citizens could engage in this activity. All this suggests production in some quantity.

Some pages in the Book of Hours from Bruges have many lines left without writing. Once in England, these were used by a professional scribe to add more prayers. These had a long rubric (i.e. instructions for use) in English. The manuscript was apparently shipped to

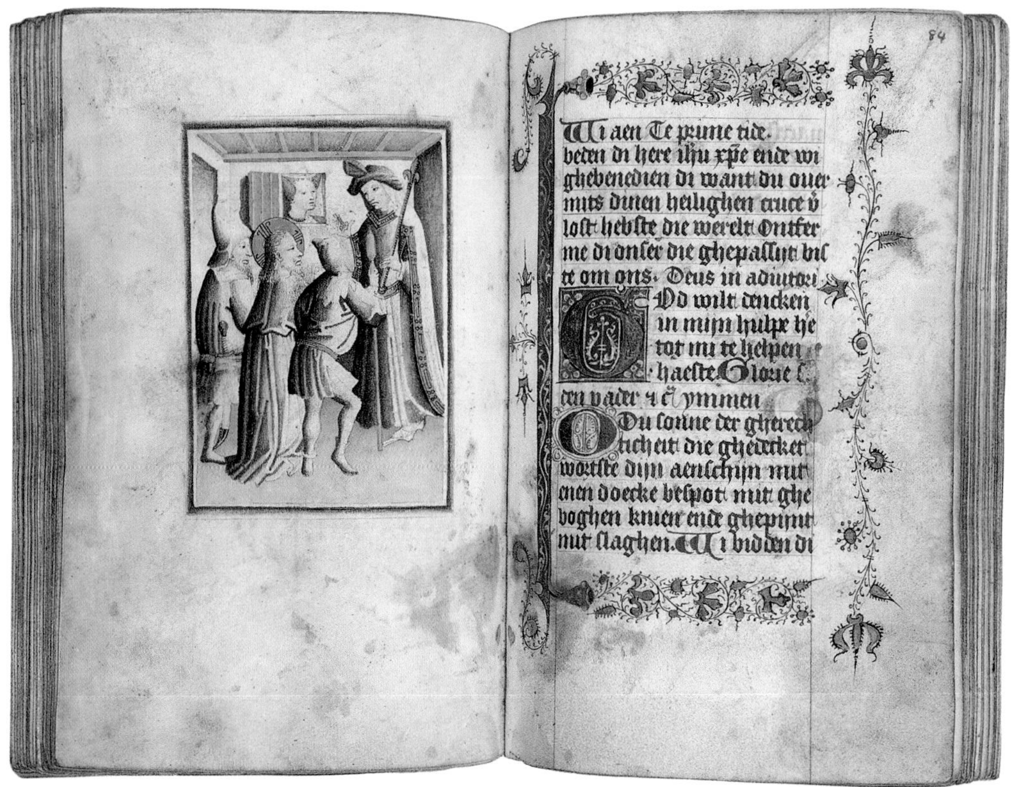

109 (left) Christ before Pontius Pilate, from a Book of Hours. Low Countries (?Delft), *c.*1440–50.

110 (above) Christ before Pontius Pilate, a print by the Master of the Gardens of Love. Low Countries. *c.*1440–50.

England in an unfinished state so that the final customer could have additions made as required.

Another group of Books of Hours shows a similar method of accelerating production. The V&A has a Book of Hours from Delft of *c.*1440–60 with a series of single-leaf illustrations bound in, all of which are painted in grisaille. They belong to a set of illustrations that were produced in some numbers: there are more than sixteen manuscripts, all of them written and decorated in different ways but all containing the same kind of miniatures. The illustrations were prepared in a completely different environment from the rest of the manuscript – bookmakers bought sets to include in Books of Hours that customers had ordered from them. The V&A manuscript (plate 109) is typical of the group, with its miniatures executed in grey washes with heavy shading, outlines in silverpoint or ink, and sparing use of yellow, light blue and occasionally gold. The compositions in manuscripts from this group are all very similar. Some kind of mechanical copying method was probably being used, although the outlines are not all identical. The image may have been transferred by tracing (tracing paper existed in the fourteenth century); if pouncing was used (i.e. dusting charcoal powder through pin-pricks that gave an outline of the image), it has left no traces. The images come from a set narrating the Passion of Christ. They were made at just the time when engraved prints were flooding on to the market, part of the climate of inventiveness that led to Gutenberg's invention of printing with movable type. The image of Christ before Pontius Pilate is close to a rather crude engraving by one of the earliest Netherlandish engravers, the Master of the Gardens of Love (active *c.*1430–45; plate 110). However, it is impossible to be certain whether the illuminators who provided these images had access to such an engraving, or whether it was the engraver who was infuenced by their work (the former appear to have had a set of models, while only a single print survives).

Towards the end of the fifteenth century, manuscript books could be replaced with facsimiles – printed books – that allowed mass production to accelerate. For the reader, these were not vastly different in appearance from what the manuscript book trade had produced. The psalter printed in Augsburg by Johann Schönsperger in 1495 looks indistinguishable from a manuscript. Its red initials were printed, but those in blue were added by

In dñicis dieb⁹ Inuitat.
Venite. Exultem⁹ dño. ps.
Venite exul. Hymnus
Nocte surgentes vi
gilemus oēs semp
in psalmis medite
mur atq̃ viribus
totis dño canamus dulciter
hymnos. Ut pio regi pari
ter canentes cū suis sctis me
reamur aulā ingredi celi sil'ꝛ
brām ducere vitā. Prestet h
nobis deitas brā p̄ris ac na
ti piterq̃ scīspūs cui⁹ reboat
in oī gl'a mūdo. Amē. In. I.
no.aii. Seruite dño. ps. I
Beatus
vir qui
nō abijt
in cōsi
lio impi
oꝝ ū ꝛ in
via pec
catoruz
nō stetit
in cathedra pestilentie non se
dit. Sed in lege dñi volūtas
ei⁹: ꝛ in lege eius meditabi
tur die ac nocte Et erit tāq̃
lignū qd plantatuz est secus
decursus aquarum: quod fru
ctuz suū dabit in tpe suo. Et
foliū eius nō defluet: ꝛ omīa
quecūq̃ faciet psperabūtur.

Non sic impij nō sic: sed tanq̃
puluis quem pijcit ventus a
facie terre Ideo nō resurgunt
impij in iudicio: neq̃ pctōres
in cōsilio iustoꝝ. Qm̄ nouit
dominus viā iustorum: ꝛ iter
impioꝝ peribit. ps. II
Quare fremuerūt gētes:
ꝛ pp'i meditati sunt in
ania Astiterūt reges tre ꝛ pnci
pes ꝯuenerūt in vnū: aduersus
dñm ꝛ aduers⁹ xpm ei⁹. Di
rūpam⁹ vincla eoꝝ: ꝛ pijciam⁹
a nob iugū ipoꝝ. Qui habi
tat in celis irridebit eos: ꝛ dñs
subsānabit eos Tūc loq̃t ad
eos i ira sua: ꝛ i furore suo cō
turbabit eos. Ego āt ꝯstitu
tus sū rex ab eo sup syō mōte
sctm ei⁹: pdicans pceptū ei⁹.
Dñs dixit ad me fili⁹ me⁹ es
tu: ego hodie genui te Postu
la a me ꝛ dabo tibi gētes here
ditatē tuam. ꝛ possessionē tuā
t'minos tre. Reges eos i vir
ga ferrea: tāq̃ vas figuli ꝯfri
ges eos. Et nūc reges itelli
gite: eru imi q iudicat terrā.
Seruite dño in timore: ꝛ ex
ultate ei cū tremore. Apphen
dite disciplinā neqñ irascatur
dñs: ꝛ peatis d via iusta Cū
exarserit in breui ira eius: bti
oēs q cōfidūt in eo. ps. III

111 Psalter, printed by Johann Schönsperger. Germany (Augsburg), 1495.

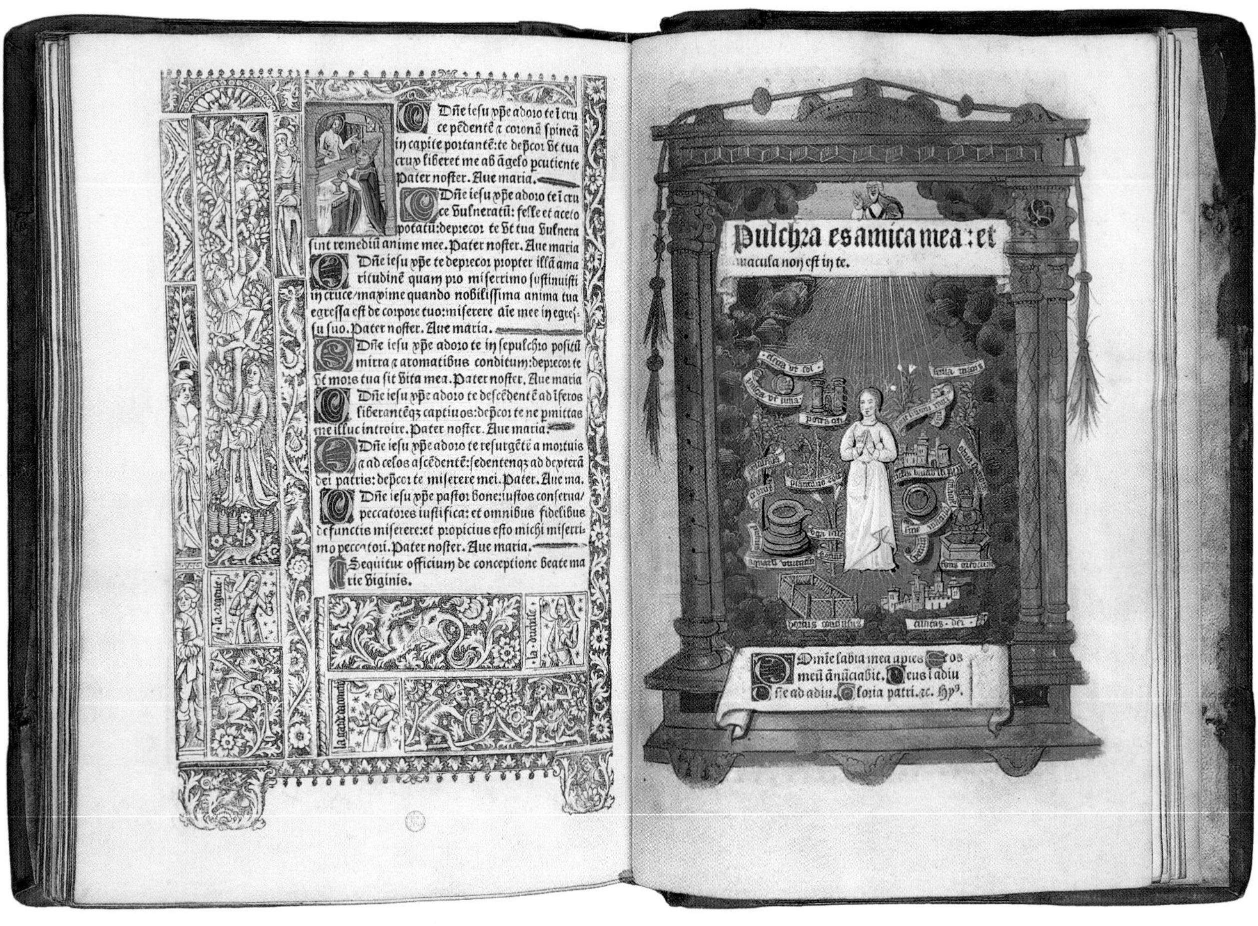

112 Book of Hours printed for Guillaume Godard. France (Paris), *c*.1510.

hand. The border illumination is in a local style; it can be paralleled, for example, in the manuscript with the Life of St Simpertus prepared for the Empeor Maximilian in 1492 (plate 111).

Books of Hours were available in printed form before 1500. The first were Italian and date from the 1470s; these usually lack ornament. By the mid-1480s, Paris had become the centre of production for Books of Hours with printed ornament, serving a Europe-wide market. Of the nearly 1,600 editions known, almost 90% came from Paris. Production figures resemble those of successful twentieth-century publishers – Guillaume Godard in 1545 had a stock of 150,000 Books of Hours. Miniatures were integral to Books of Hours, since the images were intended to guide the user's thoughts as he or she read the text. Many printed Books of Hours were illuminated by hand (colour, too, may have been a requirement of some customers). The imagery and ornament in these books became part of people's everyday visual experience. For us, they show how Renaissance design from Italy was received and recast – there are copies of antique decorative motifs but also candelabra that shelter Gothic grotesques of a traditional kind. The Italianate frame seen in an illuminated copy of of a Book of Hours printed by Guillaume Godard (plate 112) is modelled on the kinds of frame found printed in Books of Hours produced by Hardouin, Kerver and other publishers from *c.*1500. The simple style, with the shapes based on a red-ink drawing, shows illumination adapting to the necessity of rapid, serial production.

A PROCESSION OF MANUSCRIPTS

This chapter presents a selection of twenty-five manuscripts from the V&A's collection, a series of works that are notable on account of their illumination or their significance as historical documents. The chronological sequence, which stretches from the twelfth to the sixteenth century, allows some similarities to be demonstrated in works of a similar date; it also makes apparent some stark contrasts. While it shows differences in approach to the design of books, it makes no attempt to provide a systematic account of the history of book production. The bibliography will allow further investigation of the background to each manuscript.

1 Leaf from the Eadwine Psalter, Canterbury, *c.*1155–60

Around 820 a magnificent copy of the Psalms was produced in the Rheims area, densely illustrated with a series of drawings in pen. These drawings still astonish by their lively, animated character, arranged almost informally around the text on the page. This Carolingian manuscript, known as the Utrecht Psalter (from the city where it has been since 1716), contains the three Latin versions of the Psalms. It was in Canterbury from at least *c.*1000, where three copies or modernized versions of it were made. This leaf comes from one of them, a major Psalter with a prefatory portrait of the scribe Eadwine, a monk at Christ Church Canterbury *c.*1155–60. This is one of the introductory leaves to the Psalter; each leaf was divided into compartments to tell the story of King David, the author of the Psalms, and the life of Christ that was foretold by the Psalms. This was the most extensive cycle of pictures for the New Testament produced in twelfth-century England.

Though a few of the compositions are related to drawings in the Utrecht Psalter, the style owes nothing to the Carolingian manuscript. The Canterbury copy has a limited range of colours. The figures are stocky and locked in monumental poses to convey the drama of the action. The convention used for the drapery is known as 'damp fold', a version of Byzantine conventions common throughout Europe from *c.*1100. The lower part of the leaf is by a different hand, showing that more than one illuminator could work in this style.

Four leaves were probably detached from the Eadwine Psalter at some time around 1600, when Thomas Nevile, Dean of Canterbury from 1597 to 1615, gave the Psalter to Trinity College, Cambridge, where it remains today. Manuscripts of this date were not generally admired, despite the rich decoration in this particular example. However, its evident antiquity attracted those who were interested in the origins of Britain. By the nineteenth century, these leaves belonged rather oddly to the collection of William Ottley (1771–1836), who saw the High Renaissance as the summit of art. In 1838 they were described as 'Saxon work, 11th century' – a barbarian curiousity and a suitable foil to later works which showed how Giotto emancipated art and set it on a route that was to lead to Raphael and his peers.

See C.M. Kauffmann, *Romanesque Manuscripts 1066–1190*, vol. III of *A Survey of Manuscripts Illuminated in the British Isles*, ed. J.J.G. Alexander (London, 1975); *The Eadwine Psalter*, ed. M. Gibson, T.A. Heslop and R.W. Pfaff (London, 1992); *The Utrecht Psalter in Medieval Art*, ed. Koert van der Horst *et al.* (Utrecht, 1996).

2 A MID-TWELFTH-CENTURY COMMENTARY BY GILBERT DE LA PORÉE ON THE EPISTLES OF ST PAUL. POITIERS

There was a great effort of academic scholarship in the cathedral schools of the twelfth century to provide a commentary on the Bible. From about 1130, the whole of the Bible had a gloss; Gilbert de la Porée (*c.*1080–1154) further revised the gloss for the Psalms and the Epistles of St Paul. Copies of his gloss have the page layout found in the V&A leaves, with the gloss written out continuously and the biblical text in a larger script put at the appropriate place alongside. This arrangement seems rather clumsy when compared to the alternate-line layout that characterized glossed books produced in Paris, but it was consistently followed for Gilbert's text throughout Europe.

Gilbert had a dramatic career. He was Chancellor of the Cathedral Chapter at Chartres from 1126, but was in Paris from *c.*1140 before being elected Bishop of Poitiers in western France in 1142. Before the establishment of the university in Paris at the end of the twelfth century, study and teaching centred on outstanding scholars based in cathedral schools – Laon, Chartres and Paris among others – where books were produced to record their teaching. After *c.*1160 Paris came to predominate as a centre of teaching and book production, but before this date books were produced in cathedral towns: their design and decoration established the standard for the text in question. It has been argued that the books produced in the circle of Gilbert in Chartres were copied in all their aspects when this scholar migrated to Paris (this has been difficult to prove since the library at Chartres was totally destroyed in 1944), so that the first Paris copies were in fact imitations of Chartres books and their illumination.

When Gilbert went to Poitiers in 1142, however, his works were copied in books that were decorated in local styles. The V&A leaves are among these. The designs of the initials are of a kind found in manuscripts produced at this time in such centres as Limoges, Angoulême and Moissac. The neat interlace of the initial, and even the colour scheme with a bright green and rich red are in a totally different idiom from Paris works of this date. The style indicates a date in the mid-twelfth century or shortly after, which suggests that it represents textual tradition supervised by Gilbert himself.

See de Hamel, 1984; P. Stirnemann, 'Gilbert de la Porée et les livres glosés à Laon, à Chartres et à Paris', *Monde médiéval et société chartraine* (Paris, 1997).

te: in oib' gras agite. hec enim uoluntas di est in xpo ihu in omnibus uobis.

Spiritum nolite extinguere: prophetias nolite spernere. Omnia autem pbate. qd bonum est tenete: ab omni specie mala abstinete uos. Ipse aut ds pacis scificet uos per omnia: ut integer sps ur et aia et corpus sine querela in aduentu dni nri ihu xpi seruet. Fidelis e ds q uocauit nos: q etia faciet. Frs orate p nob. Salutate frs omis in osculo sco. Adiuro uos p dnm ut legat epla omib' scis fribus. Gra dni nostri ihesu xpi uobiscum amen.

PAULUS et siluanus. et thimotheus. eccle thessalonicensium: in do patre et dno ihu xpo. Gra uob et pax a do patre nro et dno ihu xpo. Gras agere sep do debem' pro uob frs ita ut dignu e. qm supercrescit fides ura. et habundat caritas uniuscuiusq; omnium urm.

inquam tria seruentur. ut sint. no dico sine pecco. quia in multis offendim' omis. s; sine querela in aduentu et c. Quod ita erit. quia ds ita futurum pmisit. qui i fa Fidelis autem e ds qui ad uitam uocauit uos. qui i fa ciet quod pmisit. Frs et c. in osculo quod dilectionis e signum. sco. no simulato. omib' scis p sacramenta. s. scificatis. Gra dni et c. amen.

Quod in precedenti epla dicit apls. mortuu in xpo in aduentu ei' resurgent primi. deinde nos q uiui m' qui residui sum' simul rapiemur cum illis. thessalonicenses n intelligentes. arbitrati sunt ante quam ipse gustaret mortem. xpm in sua maiestate uenturum. Ne g erroris hui' causa turbentur. iterum scribit eis. Et primo dicens se p illis gras age et orare. asserit quod aduentum xpi antixps pueniet. et quamuis obscura. tn aliqua aduentus eidem anti xpi signa futura denuntiat. Circa finem iterum ut curiosos corripiant. obsecrat. Paulus et c. More solito salutationem pmittit. deinde qm quicquid hnt ex deo e. agitarum actione incipit. et ait. Gras agere debemus deo puob ita ut dignum e qualis. s. collatarum dignitas exigit gratiarum. Et uere e magna. qm crescentibus tribulationib' no m no deficit. s; et supercrescit. i. magis magisq; pficit fides ura ad dnm. et habundat karitas uniuscuiusq; ad pximum inuicem ut. s. et q diligitur diligat. et mutuis obsequiis karitatem ostendat. ita ut et nos ipsi magistri uri in . i . puob bene instructis gloriemur usq; in ecclis dei. maxime p patientia ura et fide seruata in omib' que sunt de loco ad locum psecutionib' uris et tormentorum tribulationib' qs sustinetis in exemplum iusti iudicii dei. sup impios futuri. Sicut enim ait petrus. tempus e ut iudicium incipiat a domo dei. et deinde. Si inquit initium a nobis. quis finis illorum qui no credunt. Hinc enim intelligitur quom no parcatur impiis qui sunt tamq sarmenta precisa ad combustionem. quando. s. iustis no parcitur pp pficiendam purgationem. Ut digni. Ordo uerborum. Sustinetis ut digni habeamini et c. Si tamen. Qsi. dicens iudicii. addo iusti. et dicens sustinetis. appono ut digni habeamini. Recte utiq; Si tn iustum e quod uere e apud dnm et c. dnm ihu uenire

3 LEAF FROM A COPY OF PETER LOMBARD'S *SENTENCES*. PARIS, *c.*1170

Peter Lombard was one of the major biblical scholars of the twelfth century. He had been in Rheims with Gilbert de la Porée and others but was established in Paris from *c.*1134 to 1137. He completed his systematic exposition of theology, the *Sentences*, in 1152. They represented a codification of Christian doctrine and a critical view of the sources on which it rested. The organization of the *Sentences* was influenced by the work Gratian had done in Bologna for the Canon Law of the church in his *Concordia discordantium canonum*, completed shortly before. Lectures on the *Sentences* became the basis of theological teaching in Paris.

Initials of the kind that introduce the text in this manuscript were once associated with the abbey of Pontigny. In fact, the page layout and decoration bear all the marks of professional production in Paris, where, in the 1160s and 1170s, the churches of St Victor and Notre Dame de Paris made these new texts available for copying by the academic community. There had been no tradition of manuscript illumination in Paris before this.

The annotations on this leaf show that the complete book had been given to the Jesuit Collège de Clermont in Paris in 1567 by one Gilles Robert, a doctor of theology. This decorative leaf was probably torn from its parent manuscript in 1763, when the Jesuit order in France was disbanded and its goods dispersed.

See C.R. Dodwell, *The Canterbury School of Illumination, 1066–1200* (Cambridge, 1954), modified by de Hamel, 1984; Walter Cahn, *Romanesque manuscripts, the twelfth century. A Survey of Manuscripts Illuminated in France*, ed. François Avril and J.J.G. Alexander (London, 1996), vol. I, pls 211, 213 and 221; vol.II, p. 109

Collegii Paris. Soc. IESV 152

KRP.D.7

INCIPIT PROLOGUS. PROEMIUM.

Cupientes aliquid de penuria ac tenuitate nostra cum paupercula in gazofilacium domini mittere, ardua scandere, opus ultra vires nostras agere presumpsimus, consummationis fiduciam laborisque mercedem in samaritano statuentes, qui prolatis in curatione semivivi duobus denariis, supereroganti cuncta reddere professus est. Delectat nos pollicentis veritas, sed terret immensitas laboris. Desiderium hortatur proficiendi, sed dehortatur infirmitas deficiendi, quam vincit zelus domus dei.

Intentio tripertita: contra hereticos; rudibus; refugis.

Quo inardescentes fidem nostram adversus errores carnalium atque animalium hominum davitice turris clipeis munire, vel potius munitam ostendere, ac theologicarum inquisitionum abdita aperire, nec non et ecclesiasticorum sacramentorum pro modulo intelligentie nostre noticiam tradere studuimus, non valentes studiosorum fratrum votis iure resistere, eorum in Christo laudabilibus studiis lingua ac stilo nos servire flagitantium, quas bigas in nobis agitat Christi karitas. Quamvis non ambigamus omnem humani eloquii sermonem calumpnie atque contradictioni emulorum semper fuisse obnoxium.

Invectio ad hereticos.

Quia dissentientibus voluntatum motibus, dissentiens quoque fit animorum sensus, ut cum omne dictum veri ratione perfectum sit, tamen dum aliud aliis aut videtur aut complacet, veritati vel non intellecte vel offendenti impietatis error obnitatur, ac voluntatis invidia resultet. Quod deus huius seculi operatur in filiis diffidentie, qui non rationi voluntatem subiciunt, nec doctrine studium impendunt, sed in his que sompniarunt sapientie verba coaptare nituntur, non veri, sed placiti rationem sectantes. Quos iniqua voluntas non ad intelligentiam veritatis, sed ad defensionem placentium incitat, non desiderantes doceri veritatem, sed ab ea ad fabulas convertentes auditum. Quorum professio est magis placita quam docenda conquirere, nec docenda desiderare, sed desideratis doctrinam coaptare. Habent rationem sapientie in superstitione, quia fidei defectionem sequitur hypocrisis mendax, ut sit vel in verbis pietas, quam amiserit conscientia. Ipsamque simulatam pietatem omni verborum mendatio impiam reddunt, false doctrine institutis fidei sanctitatem corrumpere molientes, auriumque pruriginem sub novello sui desiderii dogmate aliis ingerentes. Qui contentioni studentes contra veritatem sine federe bellant. Inter veri namque assertionem et placiti defensionem pertinax pugna est, dum se et veritas tenet, et se voluntas erroris tuetur. Horum igitur deo hodibilem ecclesiam evertere, atque ora opilare, ne virus nequitie in alios effundere queant, et lucernam veritatis in candelabro exaltare volentes, in labore multo ac sudore volumen deo prestante compegimus ex testimoniis veritatis in eternum fundatis, in quatuor libris distinctum. In quo maiorum exempla doctrinamque reppeies. In quo per dominice fidei sinceram professionem viperee doctrine fraudulentiam prodidimus, aditum demonstrande veritatis complexi, nec periclo impie professionis inserti, temperato inter utrumque moderamine utentes. Sicubi vero vox nostra parum insonuit, non a paternis discessit limitibus. Non igitur debet hic labor cuiquam pigro vel multum docto videri superfluus, cum multis impigris multisque indoctis, inter quos etiam et mihi, sit necessarius, brevi volumine complicans patrum sententias, appositis eorum testimoniis, ut non sit querenti necesse librorum numerositatem evolvere, cui brevitas quod queritur offert sine labore. In hoc autem tractatu non solum pium lectorem, sed etiam liberum correctorem desidero, maxime ubi profunda versatur veritatis questio, que utinam tot haberet inventores, quot habet contradictores. Ut autem quod queritur facilius occurrat, titulos quibus singulorum librorum capitula distinguantur premisimus.

Explicit prologus. Incipiunt capitula primi libri.

4 A LECTERN BIBLE FROM HAINAUT(?) OF *c*.1260–1270 (THE GLAZIER-RYLANDS BIBLE)

This leaf from a large Bible in several volumes was made for a religious community rather than for a scholar. Its format shows that it was designed to lie on a lectern to be read. The illumination is of a high quality and was probably the work of itinerant illuminators whose work can be found in manuscripts produced in other centres. Where exactly the Glazier-Rylands Bible was made has been disputed. Cambrai has been proposed, as well as Tournai and the county of Hainaut. The difficulty lies in part in locating a notional workshop in a specific area, in a situation in which travelling artists were brought together for *ad hoc* commissions in different places. At least three illuminators who worked on the Bible moved on to Liège to contribute to a magnificent Psalter (Bibliothèque Nationale de France, ms latin 1077), which is considered to have introduced an up-to-date High Gothic style from France to that area.

This Bible is now scattered between several repositories, including the Glazier Collection in the Pierpont Morgan Library, New York, and the John Rylands University Library in Manchester. The leaves from the Bible now in the V&A were acquired from the dealer and scholar W.H. James Weale in 1883.

See Judith Oliver, *Gothic Manuscript Illumination in the Diocese of Liège,* c.*1250*–c.*1330*, 2 vols (Leuven, 1988)

Right: Book of Wisdom, with historiated letter *D* (Solomon and a soldier).
Left: First Book of Kings, with historiated initial *F* (an altar between Eli with gold censer and Hannah kneeling).

xpc's respondit

Si murus est: edificemus super eum propugnacula argentea. Si ostium est: compingamus illud tabulis cedrinis. Ego murus. et ubera mea sicut turris: ex quo facta sum coram eo. quasi pacem reperiens. Vinea fuit pacifico: in ea que habet populos. Tradidit eam custodibus. Vir affert pro fructu eius mille argenteos. Vinea mea coram me est. Mille tui pacifici: et ducenti hiis qui custodiunt fructus eius. Que habitas in ortis amici auscultant: fac me audire vocem tuam. Fuge dilecte mi: et assimilare capree hinnuloque cervorum super montes aromatum. Explicunt cantica canticorum. Incipit prologus in libro sapientie. Liber sapientie apud hebreos nusquam est: unde et ipse stilus grecam magis eloquentiam redolet. Hunc iudei philonis esse affirmant. Qui proinde sapientia nominatur: quia in eo xpi adventus. qui est sapientia patris. et passio evidenter exprimitur. Explicit prologus. Incipit liber Sapientie.

Respondet ecclesia.

Synagoga ecclesie dicit.

xpc dicit.

Vox xpi.

Vox ecclesie ad xpm.

Diligite iusticiam: qui iudicatis terram. Sentite de domino in bonitate: et in simplicitate cordis querite illum. Quoniam invenitur ab his qui non temptant illum: apparet autem eis qui fidem habent in illum. Perverse enim cogitationes separant a deo: probata autem virtus corripit insipientes. Quoniam in malivolam animam non introibit sapientia: nec habitabit in corpore

5 A Pocket Book of Hours. Rheims(?), *c.*1300

Medieval church services consisted of Offices, a cycle of prayers and readings throughout the day, and the Mass itself. Life in monasteries revolved around the recitation of Offices at the canonical hours of the day designated for prayer (from Matins before sunrise to Compline after dark), and the full cycle made up the Breviary. Offices devoted to the Virgin Mary developed from the tenth century. Pope Urban II (1088–99) ordered all clerics to recite them daily for the success of the First Crusade. Thereafter their popularity followed the astonishing rise of devotions to the Virgin of the later Middle Ages.

The Book of Hours, with the Office to the Virgin at its core, was an abbreviated version of a Breviary designed for use by lay people. In the twelfth and thirteenth centuries, the Psalter was the prayerbook most commonly owned by lay people. English Psalters of the fourteenth century are among the most spectacular illuminated manuscripts of the Middle Ages. A small number of thirteenth-century Books of Hours are known, many of them owned by women, and a number have a Psalter attached. This manuscript follows the Use of Rheims (i.e. the form of prayers used in that diocese), and was probably made in that region. The small format indicates that it was for private devotions, and suggests an intimate form of silent reading rather than recitation out loud.

Although Books of Hours of a later date, especially the fifteenth century, were produced to a standard pattern by the book trade, this manuscript of *c.*1300 was an individually commissioned work, with text and images possibly chosen by a cleric for the lay owner. Its first folios have a series of full-page images: apart from those recounting the Passion of Christ, there are images of John the Baptist, St Stephen, St Catherine, St Nicholas and St Christopher. This kind of prefatory cycle was soon to disappear in the fourteenth century.

The major divisions of the text are marked by historiated initials: red, blue, ochre and green predominate. The impact of the images relies on gesticulating figures whose features are drawn within an outline silhouette in a thick black line. Garments are shown as drapery with patterned folds picked out in black. The most striking aspect of the ornament is the antennae in cusped compartments on which grotesques play. This burlesque fauna, though known in thirteenth-century Paris, is particularly characteristic of northern France, Flanders and England in the last years of the thirteenth century.

See *L'Art au temps des rois maudits: Philippe le Bel et ses fils, 1285–1328* (Paris, 1998) for an account of regional schools in north-eastern France around 1300.

Top: ff.47v–48 Presentation at the Temple.
Bottom: ff.53v–54 Massacre of the Innocents and grotesques.

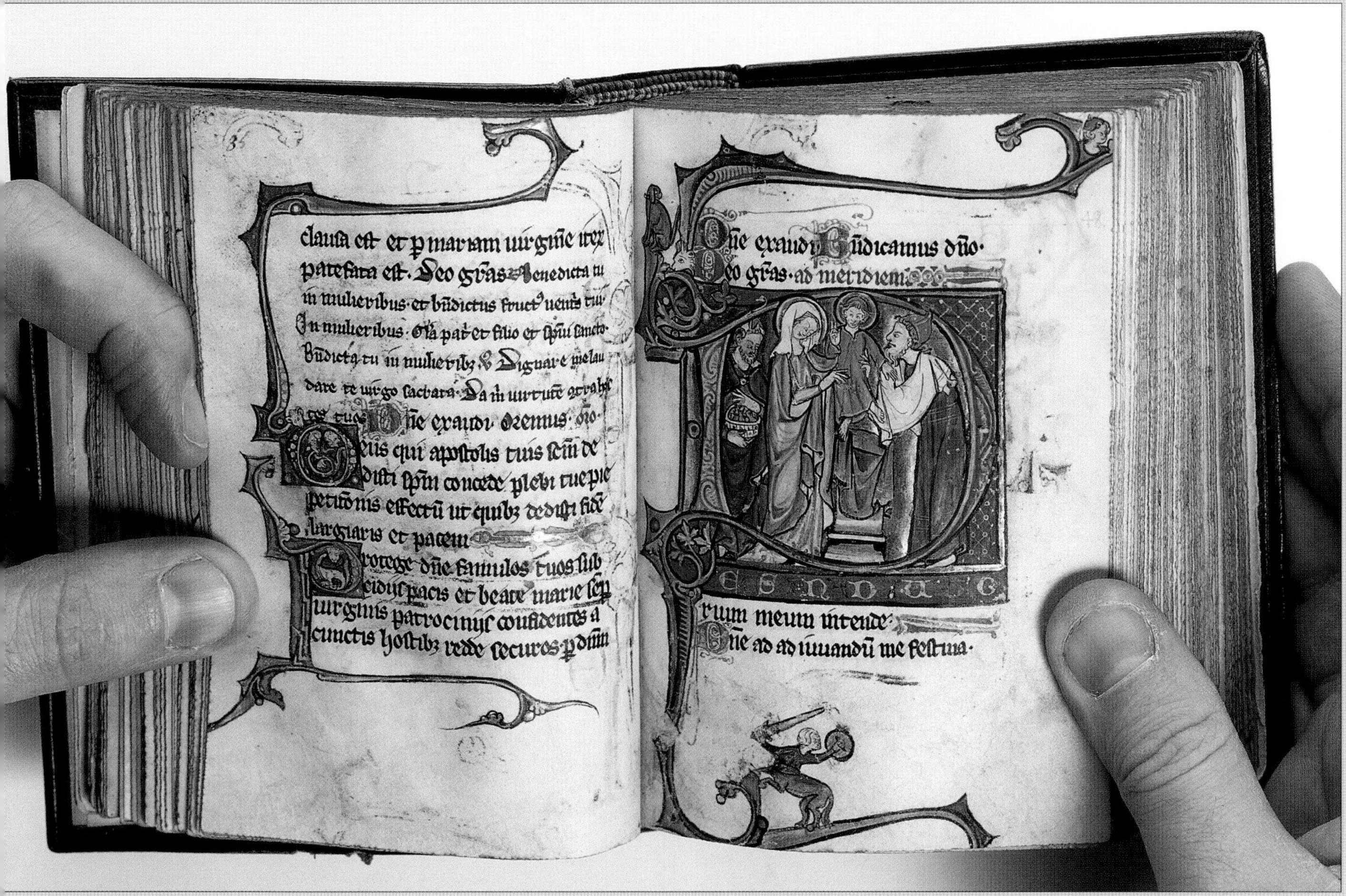

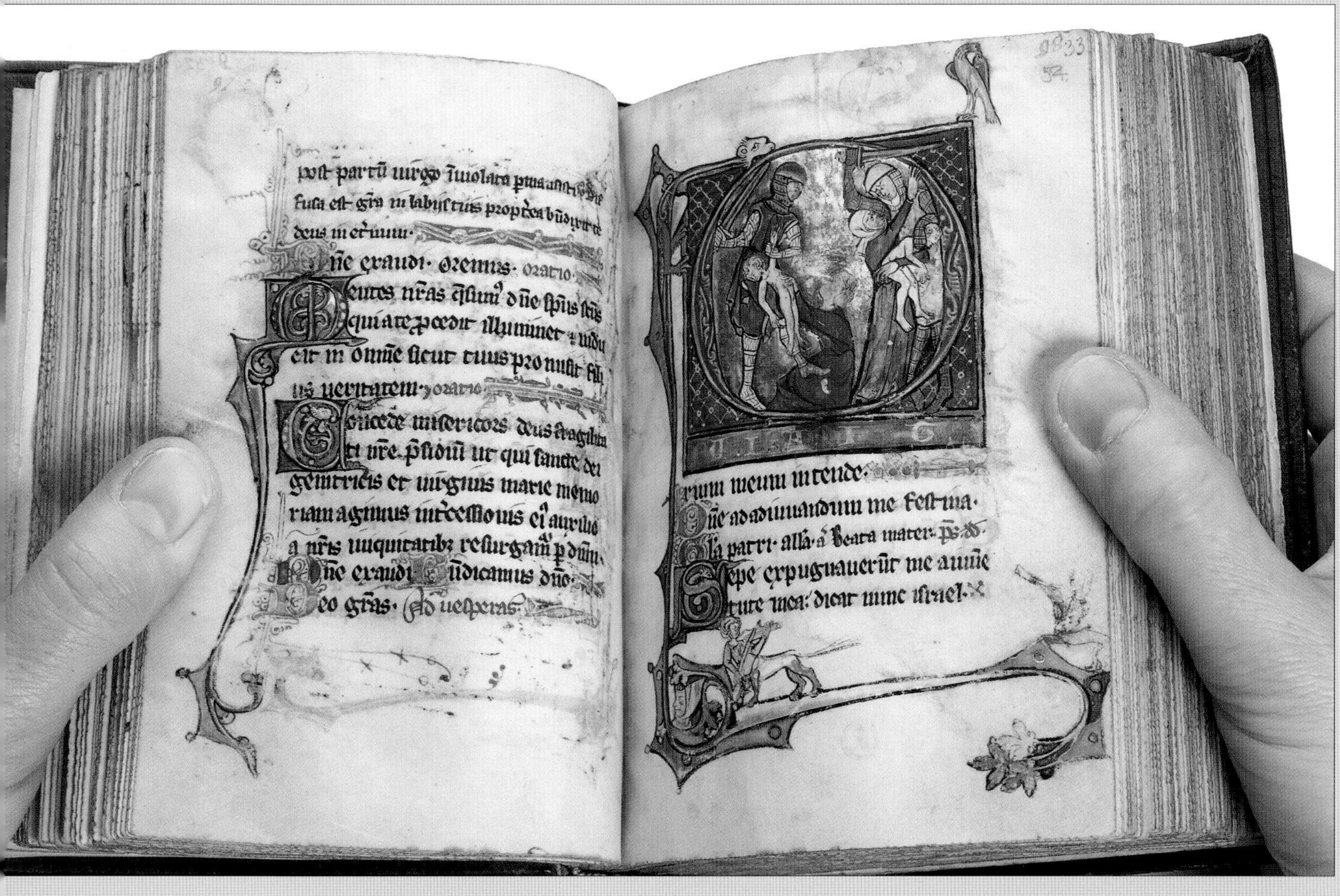

clausa est et p mariam uirgiñe iterũ
patefacta est. Deo gras. Benedicta tu
in mulieribus et bñdictus fruct' uentris tui.
In mulieribus. Gl'a patri et filio et sp̃ui sancto.
Bñdicta tu in mulierib3. Dignare me lau
dare te uirgo sacrata. Da m uirtutẽ 9tra hos
tes tuos. Dñe exaudi. Oremus. Oro.
Deus qui apostolis tuis scm̃ de
disti sp̃m concede plebi tue pie
peticõnis effectũ ut quibz dedisti fidē
largiaris et pacem.
Protege dñe famulos tuos sub
sidiis pacis et beate marie sep
uirginis patrociniis confidentes a
cunctis hostibz redde securos. p dñm.

Dñe exaudi. Bñdicamus dño.
Deo gras. ad meridiem.
rium meum intende.
Dñe ad adiuuandũ me festina.

post partũ uirgo inuiolata pmansisti. Dif
fusa est gr̃a in labiis tuis propt'ea bñdixit te
deus in et'num.
Dñe exaudi. Oremus. Oratio.
Mentes nr̃as q̃sum dñe sp̃us sc̃us
qui a te pcedit illuminet & indu
cat in omnẽ sicut tuus pro misit fili
us ueritatem. Oratio.
Concede misericors deus fragilitati
nr̃e. p̃sidiũ ut qui sancte dei
genitricis et uirginis marie memo
riam agimus intercessionis ei' auxilio
a nr̃is iniquitatib3 resurgam' p dñm.
Dñe exaudi. Bñdicamus dño.
Deo gras. Ad uesperas.

rium meum intende.
Dñe ad adiuuandum me festina.
Gl'a patri. alla. a' Beata mater. ps.
Sepe expugnauerũt me a iuuẽ
tute mea: dicat nunc israel.

6 The Teutonic Knights Bible. Liège, early fourteenth century

The Teutonic Knights were among the more successful military orders. They were given papal approval in 1199 and oversaw the colonization by German settlers and the imposition of Christianity in what is now Poland and Lithuania. Like their counterparts, the Templars, who suffered the brutal suppression and nationalization of their assets by the French crown just after 1300, they operated a system of banking to get money 'to the front line'. This Bible was made in Liège for their house of Nieuwe Biesen in Maastricht, where the order owned property. The illumination relies on an ornamental vocabulary of interlaced and spiral stems (similar to those of the twelfth and early thirteenth century but with three-pointed leaves rather than acanthus sprays) inhabited by dragons, heads and grotesques. The palette is dominated by blue, brick red and orange red, with some dark green. The rather restrained antennae that issue from initials into the margins support grotesques and animals. Above the eager dog (below) can be seen what is either a preparatory drawing or a copy of the outline.

This Bible was originally in three volumes. The last volume is today in Keble College, Oxford, while fragments from the other two are in the British Library and the V&A, both acquired from W.H. James Weale.

See Judith Oliver, *Gothic Manuscript Illumination in the Diocese of Liège,* c.*1250*–c.*1330*, 2 vols (Leuven, 1988); M.B. Parkes, *The Medieval Manuscripts of Keble College, Oxford* (Scolar Press, 1979), MS 69.

Right: Prologue to Book of Esther, with decorated initials and grotesques.
Left: Book of Hosea (detail).

festiuitas ab hebreis in numero die
rum sanctorum accipitur et colitur
a iudeis ex illo tempore usq; in pre
sentem diem.

Explicit liber Judith. Incipit p
logus ieronimi in librū hester.

Librū hes
ter uariis
transla
toribus
constat
esse uicia
tum. quē
ego de ar
chiuis he
breorum
releuans.
uerbo e uerbo expressius transtuli. Quē
librum editio uulgata laciniosis hinc
inde uerborū funibus trahit. addens
ea que ex tempore dici poterant et au
diri. sicut solitum est scolaribus disci
plinis sumpto themate excogitare qb'
uerbis uti potuit qui iniuriam pass'
est: uel ille qui iniuriam fecit. Vos
autem o paula et eustochium. quoni
am bibliothecas hebreorum studuistis
intrare. et interp̄tum certamina com
probastis. tenentes hester hebraicum
librum per singula uerba nostrā trāsl
lationē aspicite. ut possitis agnoscere
me nichil etiam augmentasse adden
do. sed fideli testimonio sīpliciter sicut
in hebreo; habetur hystoria hebraicā la
tine lingue tradidisse. Nec affectamus
laudes hominū. nec uituperationes ex
pauescimus. Deo enim placere curan
tes minas hominū penitus non time
mus. quoniā dissipat deus ossa eorū
qui hominibus placere desiderāt. et se
cundum apostolum qui huiusmodi sc̄
serui xp̄i esse non possunt. Rursum
alfabetum in libro hester ex minio usq;
ad thetam litteram fecimus diuersis
in locis uolentes scilicet septuaginta
interp̄tum ordinem per hec insinuare
studioso lectori. Nos enim iuxta mo
rem hebreum ordinem prosequi etiā
in septuaginta editione maluimus.
Explicit prologus. Incipit liber hest'.

I
In diebus assueri qui regnauit
ab india usq; ethyopiam super
centū uiginti et septem prouinci
as quando sedit in solio regni
sui. susa ciuitas regni eius exor
dium fuit. Tercio igitur anno
imperii sui fecit grande conui
uium cunctis p̄ncipibus et pu
eris suis fortissimis. persarum
et medorum inclitis et p̄fectis
prouinciarū coram se. ut osten
deret diuicias glorie regni sui:
et magnitudinē atq; iactanciā
potencie sue. multo tempore cen
tum uidelicet et octoginta dieb'.
Cumq; implerentur dies conui
uii inuitauit omnē populum
qui inuentus est susis a maxi
mo usq; ad minimū: et septem
diebus iussit conuiuiū parari
in uestibulo orti et nemoris. qd
regio cultu et manu consitum
erat. Et pendebant ex ōi parte
tentoria aerei coloris et carbasi
ni. et iacinctini sustentata funi

7 An Antiphoner from the Franciscan Convent of St Klara. Cologne, *c.*1350

The Antiphoner contained the choral parts for the cycle of Offices celebrated by a monastic or other community; its size enabled the whole choir to read the music at once. This Antiphoner was made at the convent of St Klara in Cologne by one of the nuns, Sister Loppa de Speculo. Another surviving leaf records that Sister Jutta paid for it, and Loppa carried out the writing, 'lining' (putting in the staves for music), notation and illumination, 'in the year 1350, when there was a great plague everywhere'. This was one of a series of books produced in the convent. The abbess, Heylwigis von Beechoven, who had ruled the convent since 1344, is portrayed kneeling by the historiated initial of the Descent of the Holy Ghost on the Virgin and Apostles, associating her prayer with this crucial event, when the Holy Spirit came to earth and the mission of the Apostles to spread the Christian revelation began. The prayer of her convent was thus part of the mission.

If we take at face value the claim that Sister Loppa did all the illumination (it is always possible that parts of it were contracted out, paid for by Sister Jutta), it appears that grotesques and birds (a heron seems to be shown) were the accepted form of ornament even in this convent environment. The initial looks German, but the three-pointed leaves on their swirling stems may show an effort to copy Parisian or other French styles. Other leaves from this manuscript are in Stockholm and in Cologne itself, collected by the founders of the Wallraf-Richartz Museum who wanted to assemble works to show the antiquity of a local school of painting.

See Sabine Benecke, *Randgestaltung und Religiosität: Die Handschriften aus dem Kölner Kloster St Klara* (Hamburg, 1995)

a templo scto tuo qd est in iheru
salem alleuia alla. ps Cruc. de.
Emitte spiritu tuum et creabi
tur et renouabis faciem terre alle
luia alla. ps Benedic.
Iste tres ant
Dum complerentur di
es penthecostes
tes e rant omnes pa riter

8 A Missal from the Royal Abbey of St Denis. Paris, *c.*1350

Apart from its other qualities, this Missal is notable in that it can be dated with some precision. The prefatory calendar mentions the death of every French king from Robert (d.20 July 1031), but not that of Philip VI, who died on 22 August 1350. On the other hand, the death of Guido of Châtres, Abbot of St Denis, on 22 February 1350 gets an entry. The probable dating is thus between 22 February 1350 and 22 August 1350, for the text at least.

The tactile qualities of the manuscript are wonderful: the parchment is light and supple, and it sits open easily, even in its eighteenth-century binding. The secondary ornament is very carefully executed – the penwork flourishing may even be by the associate of Jean Pucelle (d.1333/4) Jacques de Macy, who appears to have specialized in this work. The ornament that runs down the left-hand of the column is finely executed; the initials and frame border reveal the quality of commercial work done by the Paris book trade.

Above: f.242 Beginning of the Sanctorale, with historiated initial D (St Andrew). Right: ff.256v-257 Feast of the Dedication of St Denis, with miniature (Christ dedicating the abbey).

The miniatures are executed by an exceptional hand. It has been identified as that of the illuminator of a de luxe copy of the poem 'Remède de fortune' by Guillaume de Machaut, the outstanding poet of fourteenth-century France. Known as the Remède de Fortune Master, he contributed to several major commissions, including a large illustrated Bible made for King Jean le Bon (r.1350–64). In the miniatures of the St Denis Missal, the figures are executed in the grisaille that Pucelle had introduced into French illumination (in the Jeanne d'Evreux Hours, see p. 48), and are modelled in the round rather than relying on an outline to show their form. The costumes are done realistically in that they match other representations of fashionable clothes of the time. The birds and butterflies in the marginal ornament show a similar realistic ambition (owls, great-tits and cranes can be identified). Apparently taking their cue from Pucelle's work, some scenes attempt to represent pictorial depth on the flat surface of the page. Spatial recession relies for its effect on the rather clumsy device of columns thrown forward in front of figures. There is some success, however, in showing recession in buildings and landscapes. It seems clear that this master had had some contact with Pucelle or people who worked with him. He demonstrates similar interests, and his skill is beyond question.

Two openings give an account of the founding and dedication of the monastery. Before its consecration, a pilgrim with leprosy spent a night in the abbey and observed Christ himself with St Denis and others consecrating the church. At the bottom of the page, Christ removes the leprous face from the pilgrim. When the king arrived, the pilgrim told him that the abbey was already consecrated and that Christ had healed him, pointing to his leprous face as proof.

The Missal was owned by Ferry de Clugny when bishop of Tournai (1473–80). He was made a cardinal in 1480 and died in Rome in 1483. The binding shows that the volume was in France in the eighteenth century. When the V&A acquired the manuscript in 1891, it had been in a collection in Cork. Although the director of the V&A asked for the manuscript to be disbound, so that individual leaves could be shown separately, the librarian, W.H. James Weale, did not permit this.

See Avril, 1978; *Les Fastes du gothique: le siècle de Charles V*, exh. cat. (Paris, Grand Palais, 1981); Anne Walters Robertson, *The Service Books of the Royal Abbey of Saint-Denis: Images of Ritual and Music in the Middle Ages* (Oxford: Clarendon Press, 1991)

Tu es pe trus et super hanc
pe tram edifica bo
ecclesi am me am
et porte inferi
non prevalebunt adver
sus e am et tibi da bo
claves regni celo
Tu es petrus et super
hanc petram edificabo ec
clesiam me am.
Terribilis est locus
iste hic domus dei est
et porta celi et voca

9 Choirbook illuminated by Silvestro dei Gherarducci for San Michele a Murano in Venice. Florence, 1392–99

Santa Maria degli Angeli in Florence, a monastery of the Camaldolese order, was the home of a number of scribes, painters and illuminators in the fourteenth and fifteenth centuries. They worked both for their own house and for other churches and even secular customers. The Italian artist and art historian Vasari (1511–74) described their work and mentioned that Pope Leo X (r.1513–21) would have taken the abbey's choirbooks to Rome if they had been usable for the Roman liturgy. Silvestro dei Gherarducci (1339–99) was active as a painter and illuminator in the abbey from the 1370s. This was not a full-time activity since he was sub-prior and then prior from 1398, both demanding administrative posts.

He illuminated works not only for Santa Maria degli Angeli but also for a Camaldolese house in Venice, San Michele a Murano. At this time, Venice was not a centre of illumination. In 1401, when Dominican nuns there wanted advice on the making of books for liturgical purposes, a Dominican from Florence, Giovanni Dominici, told them to study the choirbooks he had seen in San Michele, which contained Silvestro's work. Illuminators such as Belbello of Pavia and Cristoforo Cortese were later employed on the San Michele choirbooks, and it is through their careers in Venice that compositions and styles developed by Silvestro dei Gherarducci became used in the city.

The V&A leaf (right) contains the initial *S* for the beginning of the Mass for Pentecost. In the upper register, the Virgin prays with the Apostles as the Holy Ghost descends; in the lower, the elders of all nations (carefully differentiated by their costume) wait for enlightenment. In the margin there is fleshy acanthus linked by long straight stems that are quite unlike the standard convention of Bolognese ornament. The panel of text (*[S]PIRITUS DO[MINI]*) has highlights delicately executed in white, rather like penwork flourishing. Silvestro may have worked as part of a team, with some of the ornament done by others. Whether or not he painted all the miniatures has been questioned. The historiated initial *A* for the Mass for Easter Tuesday (left), with its bearded prophet holding a scroll, has been attributed to an assistant named the Master of the Canzoni. The hand seems slightly clumsy, but the illuminator is clearly working in the same style as Silvestro dei Gherarducci.

See Laurence B. Kanter *et al.*, *Painting and Illumination in Early Renaissance Florence, 1300–1450* (New York, 1994); Mirella Levi d'Ancona, *The Choirbooks of Santa Maria degli Angeli in Florence*, 2 vols (Florence, 1993 and 1994)

PIRITUS·DO

In illo tempore: Cum
natus esset ihc in beth
leem iude in diebus
Herodis regis: ecce ma

10 A Book of Hours. Paris, *c.*1410–15

By the end of the fourteenth century, the Paris book trade was highly organized, working under the aegis of the University of Paris. Apart from providing books (new and second-hand) needed by academics, lawyers and administrators, it also supplied the de luxe market. The V&A manuscript, a product of this environment, contains ten miniatures (ten more were probably removed by nineteenth-century collectors), of which all but one are in the style of the Boucicaut Master, whose masterpiece was a Book of Hours done for the Maréchal de Boucicaut in around 1405–8. The colours are rich; tall, gracefully posed figures are contained in roomy spaces. There are the conventional diapered grounds of fourteenth-century tradition, but also landscape backgrounds with deep blue skies that get lighter towards the horizon, as well as townscapes. It has been suggested that the Boucicaut Master was Jacques Coene, a Flemish painter who worked in Paris and spent some time in 1399 in Milan to work on the cathedral.

The other miniaturist in the V&A manuscript is known as the Egerton Master, identified by a manuscript from the Egerton Collection in the British Library. The colouring here is less subtle, though the face is more carefully modelled with pigment. The Evangelist portrayed sits against a vermiculated ground of a traditional type (one often used by miniaturists associated with the Boucicaut style). Whereas the border ornament of the Boucicaut-type pictures consists of thin stem spirals (again, found elsewhere associated with Boucicaut-style miniatures), that for the Egerton picture is of fleshy acanthus in spirals that harbour small figurative scenes. Borders of this kind reflect an attempt to copy Italian examples, and their appearance in the Paris book trade is associated with the so-called Brussels Initials Master.

The exact relationship between this manuscript and those classed as issuing from the Boucicaut workshop is unclear. It belongs to one of two groups linked with works thought to be by the Boucicaut Master or directed by him, but it evidently reflects the kind of co-operative working practices and *ad hoc* participation to fulfil a client's order on which the Paris book trade depended.

See Meiss, 1968; François Avril, Marie-Thérèse Gousset, Jacques Monfrin *et al.*, *Marco Polo: Das Buch der Wunder: Handschrift français 2810 der Bibliothèque Nationale de France, Paris*, 2 vols (Lucerne, 1996). On the image of the Nativity in this manuscript, see R. Schilling, 'The Nativity and the adoration of the Child Christ in French miniatures of the early fifteenth century', *Connoisseur*, vol. CXXX (1952), pp. 167–69

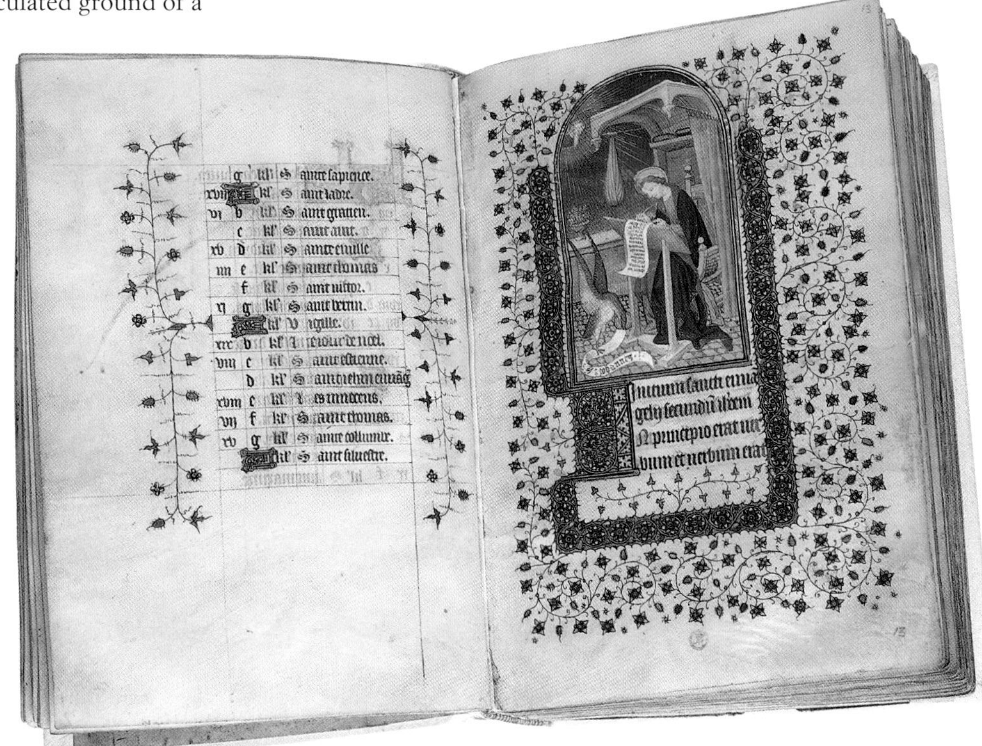

Left: f.16 Gospel extracts: St Matthew.
Right: ff.12v–13 End of calendar and beginning of Gospel extracts: St John.

11 Miniatures by the Dunois Master from a Book of Hours. Paris, *c*.1450

The Dunois Master was once known as 'The principal associate of the Bedford Master'. The Bedford Master took his name from two outstanding manuscripts made for John of Lancaster, Duke of Bedford and brother of Henry V, victor at Agincourt in 1415. Bedford ruled lands conquered in France for the infant Henry VI from 1422 to 1435, and based his government in Paris. The Bedford Master's style was widely practised in Paris, so much so that manuscripts have been categorized as by the Master, by his associate, by his workshop and by followers, with a large number being designated as representing the 'Bedford Trend'. The Dunois Master appears to have adopted most closely the painting style and models of the Bedford Master; his latest works are datable to the 1460s, by which time they have a distinctly old-fashioned look.

Most of the Dunois Master's works were apparently for powerful aristocrats. Apart from work for Jean d'Orléans, Count of Dunois, he illuminated a Book of Hours for a member of the Jouvenel des Ursins family. Of bourgeois origins, members of the family became Archbishop of Rheims and Chancellor of France in the 1450s. The V&A leaves come from a Book of Hours made for an unidentified member of the family (the device of a bear's foot – *ours* in French – is found in the ornament of another leaf from the manuscript).

The miniatures reveal the dramatic narrative thrust for which the Bedford Master is noted. St Giles is shown in the lower margin in the forest with his companion, a hind, discovered in their solitude by the king's hunters – Giles then consents to found a monastery for the king. When out hunting, St Julian is told by a deer that he will murder his parents, while in the lower margin he is about to slay his parents in bed, thinking that the woman is his wife with a lover. The figures are exquisitely painted in white, probably evocative of enamelled goldsmiths' work for contemporary readers. As in many works associated with the Dunois Master, the text is in a small 'bastard' script (see p. 14), doubtless marking the taste of the connoisseurs for whom the books were made.

See François Avril and Nicole Reynaud, *Les Manuscrits à peintures en France, 1440–1520* (Paris, 1993)

Above: Scene from the life of St Giles.
Right: Scenes from the life of St Julian.

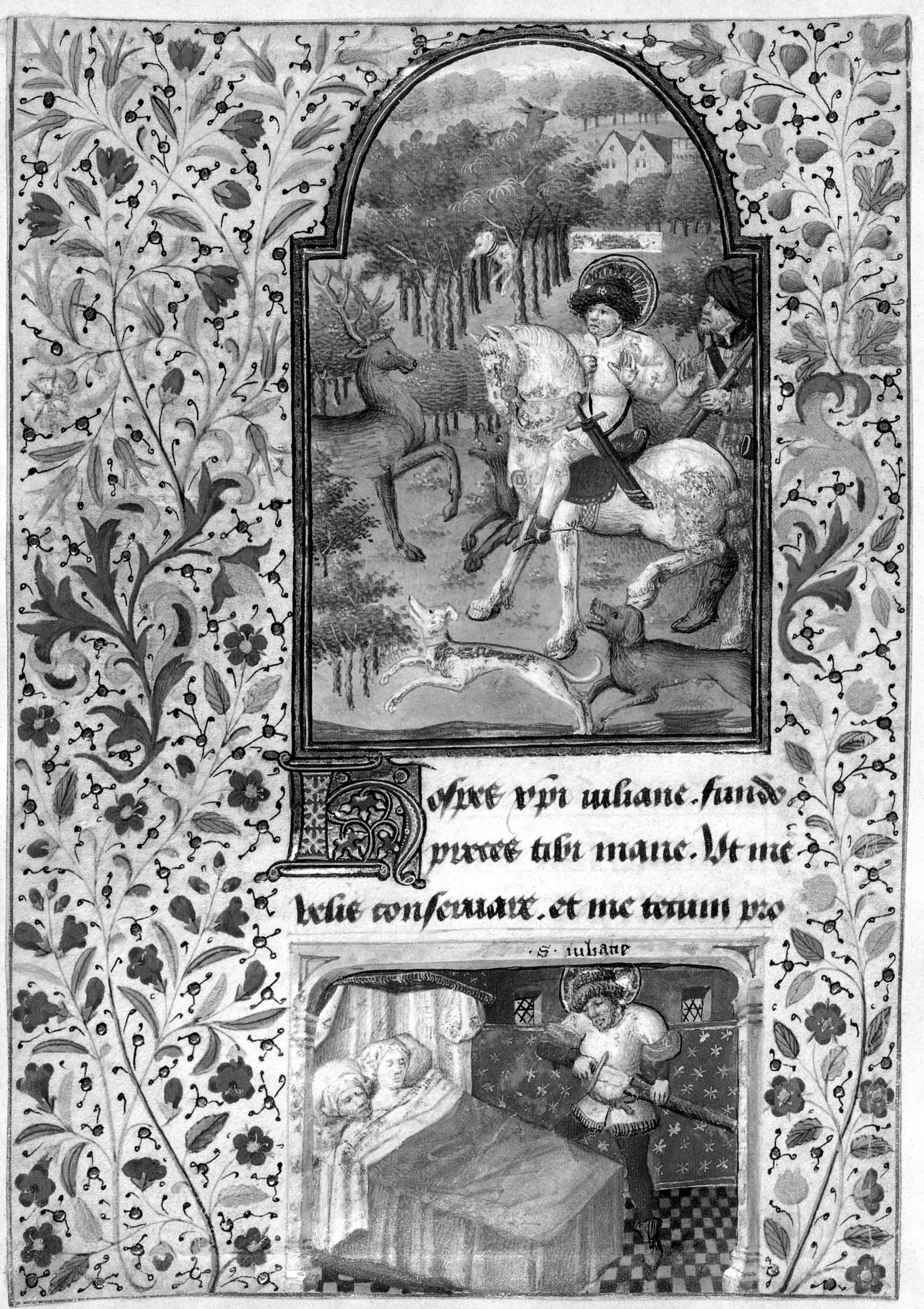

Hospes xpi iuliane. fundo
preces tibi mane. Ut me
velis conservare. et me tutum pro
·S· iuliane

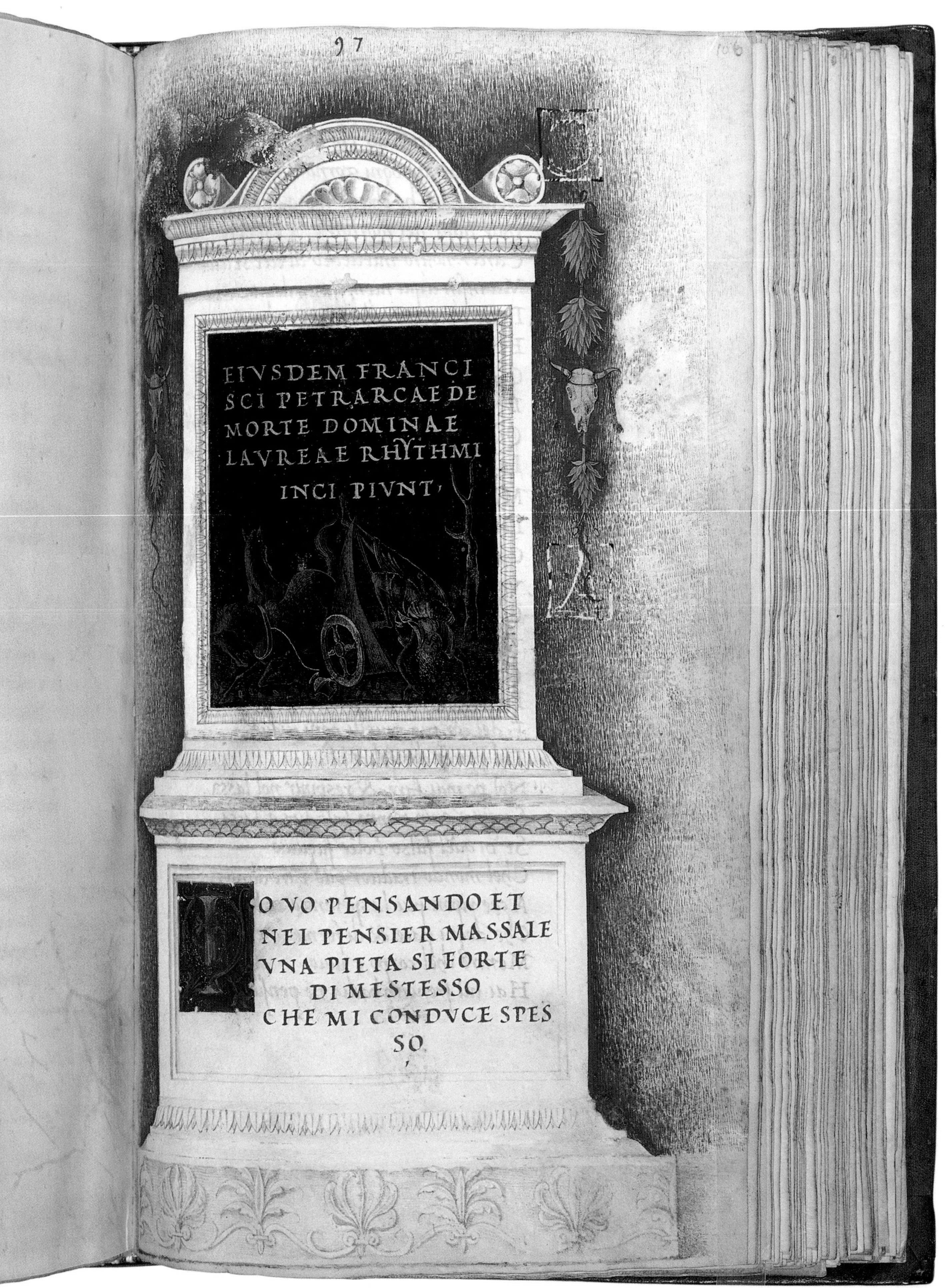
EIVSDEM FRANCI
SCI PETRARCAE DE
MORTE DOMINAE
LAVREAE RHYTHMI
INCI PIVNT.
O VO PENSANDO ET
NEL PENSIER MASSALE
VNA PIETA SI FORTE
DI MESTESSO
CHE MI CONDVCE SPES
SO.

12 The Sanvito Petrarch. Padua, mid- or late 1460s

In a much-quoted eulogy to the scholar Ciriaco d'Ancona, the antiquary and poet Felice Feliciano described a boating trip on 23 and 24 September 1464 around Lake Garda in which he took part with the painters Mantegna and Samuele da Tradate, and the engineer Giovanni da Padova. Their aim was to study classical monuments and the inscriptions on them. This enthusiasm for Roman remains expressed itself in the collecting of antiquities of all kinds, from sculpture to gems and coins, from inscriptions to classical texts. It is just this world – the archaeological phase of the Renaissance – that informs this copy of a non-classical text, the *Rime e trionfi* (*Sonnets and Triumphs*) of Petrarch. It was written out by the celebrated scribe Bartolomeo Sanvito, in his italic script; he also added to it the faceted initials that appealed to classical enthusiasts of the day.

The illumination is the work of two miniaturists. One worked on sheets of parchment stained yellow and purple, in imitation of Carolingian and late classical manuscripts. The second part of the sonnets (left) has an introductory image, again a funerary monument, representing the death of Laura. The purple sheet (below) is the preface to the *Trionfi* of Petrarch; the title is inscribed on a classical plinth, while a king, his hands bound behind his back, walks in front of a carriage bearing Cupid with a bow and arrow, surrounded by figures with hands similarly tied to signify their submission to love. The architectural frame matches that for the beginning of the sonnets.

The first artist has not been identified, but the range of his knowledge of Antique works demonstrates prolonged study of classical sources. The image of Laura's death, for instance, was copied from a Roman tomb sculpture. The second artist was probably Franco dei Russi – the V&A recently acquired a signed cut-out initial by this illuminator, one of two known today, which supports the identification (E.1275-1991). A cardinal's hat has been painted over the miniature on f.9v: this has been variously attributed to Ludocvico Trevisan (d.1465) and to Francesco Gonzaga (1444–83). The inventory of Gonzaga's estate taken after his death refers to a Petrarch 'bound in green silk', and there are indeed traces of green textile underneath the magnificent binding of 1515–25 done in Rome. Trevisan owned other manuscripts bearing the work of both Sanvito and Franco dei Russi.

See J.J.G. Alexander, 'A manuscript of Petrarch's *Rime* and *Trionfi*', *Victoria and Albert Museum Yearbook*, vol. II (1970), pp. 27–40; J.J.G. Alexander, ed., *The Painted Page: Italian Renaissance Book Illumination, 1450–1550* (Munich and New York, 1994); *Miniature a Padova* (Padua, 1999)

Left: f.106 Classical tomb monument with an allegorical image of the death of Laura. Right: ff.149v–150 On parchment stained purple, the Triumph of Love, a crowned figure leading a chariot with a putto about to fire a flaming arrow; opposite, an architectural frame with the beginning of the poem.

13 Book of Hours made for Galeazzo di Sanseverino and later owned by Alfonso of Aragon. Naples, *c.*1470–80

Alfonso of Aragon was Duke of Calabria from 1458, a brutal soldier whose collecting of art objects and manuscripts was probably directed by his officials more than by his own taste. His grandfather Alfonso I had assembled one of the most prestigious libraries in Italy, which was developed by his illegitimate son Ferrante I, king from 1458 to 1494. Alfonso I had been praised in the autobiography of the celebrated Florentine bookseller Vespasiano da Bisticci (see p. 11). This manuscript was produced for a minor figure, Galeazzo, the youngest brother of the Robert di Sanseverino (d.1474), a companion-in-arms of the king who made him Prince of Salerno in 1463. (Robert is not to be confused with his relation of the same name from the family that served as mercenaries of the Sforza duke of Milan at this time. This Robert had a son named Galeazzo, suggesting that it corresponded to some family tradition.) It appears that the manuscript was confiscated by Alfonso of Aragon when he suppressed – with characteristic bloodthirstiness – the barons' revolt of 1485–86. Several books are known to have entered the royal library by this route; in this case the arms of Alfonso were painted over those of Galeazzo.

This Book of Hours is a large, luxury object (Books of Hours were being printed in Naples at this time, but they were pocket-size). The illumination is by Matteo Felice, who is known from archival sources to have worked for the king and wealthy citizens between 1467 and 1483. The ornament of the illuminated pages is very finely worked. The Annunciation miniature with its sharply receding corridor between two buildings echoes a composition that was current in Florence in the 1460s. The white-vine marginal ornament is inhabited by cherubs and animals, a design that was rather old-fashioned by this date. A series of miniatures tells the story of the taking of Jerusalem by the Emperor Titus. It was once considered to have encouraged Alfonso to emulate the Roman Emperor, but it seems rather that the crusading ideal it implied was common to the baronial and royal classes.

See Tammaro de Marinis, *La biblioteca napoletana dei re d'Aragona*, vol. I (Milan, 1952); J.J.G. Alexander, ed., *The Painted Page: Italian Renaissance Book Illumination, 1450–1550* (Munich and New York, 1994); Gennaro Toscano, 'Matteo Felice: un miniatore al servizio dei re d'Aragona di Napoli', *Bolletino d'Arte*, nos 93–94 (1995/6)

Left: ff.335v-336 Office of Trinity Sunday: miniature with Abraham receiving three angels.
Right: f.14 Annunciation.

Incipit officiū beate Marie virginis
secundum cōsuetudinē Romane cu
rie. Ad matutinum. versus.
Domine labia mea aperies
Et os meum annūciabit la
udem tuam. V. Deus in adiutoriū
meum intende. R. Domine ad adiuuan
dum me festina. Gloria pr̄i et filio. Sicut
Inuitat. Aue Maria gratia plena Dñs tecū
Venite exultemus domino in

14 The Book of Hours of Margaret de Foix. Rennes, 1471–76

This manuscript was made for Margaret de Foix (d.1487), wife of François II, Duke of Brittany (b.1435, r.1458–88). This appears from a careful reading of the erased coats of arms to be found in the book (Brittany with Foix), and from the prayer added at the end of the text (in a different hand and with different ornament) asking for the end of the sterility of the marriage. Since the couple married in July 1471 and had their first child, Anne de Bretagne, in January 1477, it seems safe to date the manuscript between 1471 and 1476.

Though the text follows the liturgical use of Paris, the manuscript was probably made in Brittany. The illumination has been linked with several works associated with Rennes, and though the quality of the painting in the V&A manuscript is rather better than these, this seems a likely location. The illustrations for the Hours of the Virgin are an odd mixture of scenes from the Passion of Christ and the story of his birth. Some consist of multiple scenes in architectural niches, but most impressive are single-page compositions such as the Nativity. In the latter, the sense of space around the kneeling Virgin and her broad cascade of drapery show similar interests to those of Fouquet in the Etienne Chevalier Hours – it is as if the illuminator was used to the more ample dimensions of panel painting (the scene of Joseph leading Mary on an ass to the inns of Bethlehem shows the relegation of the anecdotal detail that is crammed into compositions elsewhere in the manuscript). The borders in the Margaret de Foix Hours are extremely rich, and rely for their effect on acanthus sprays with flowers and fruit (the varieties are recognizable by schematized rather than realistic depiction), and the usual range of animals and grotesques. There are three distinct border styles: the opening with the image of St Anthony has two of them, perhaps the work of two separate illuminators.

See J.P. Harthan, *Books of Hours* (London, 1977); E. König, *Französische Buchmalerei um 1450* (Berlin, 1982), with many illustrations; *La Bretagne au temps des ducs* (Daoulas, 1991)

Top: ff.208v–209 St Anthony.
Bottom: ff.60v–61 Nativity.

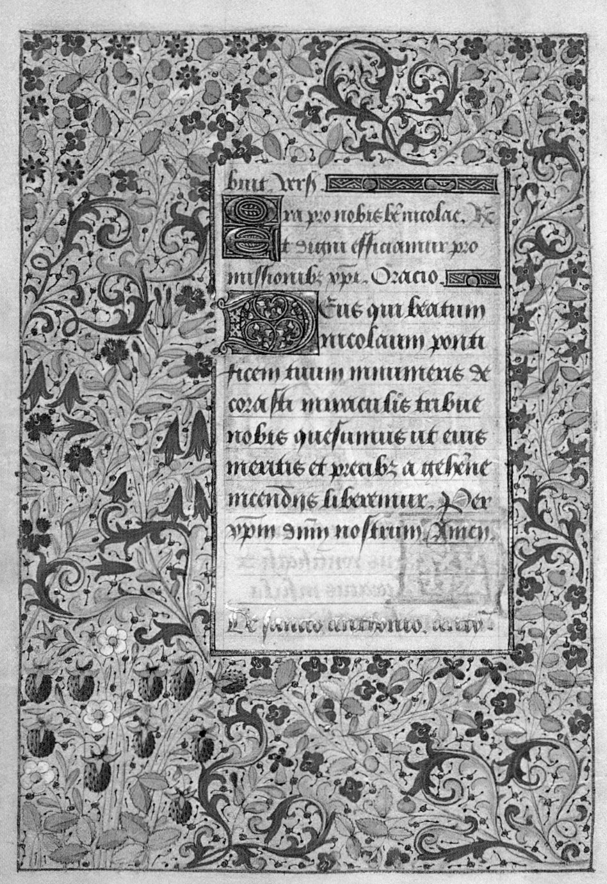
buit. Vers.
Ora pro nobis be nicolae.
Ut digni efficiamur pro
missionibus xpi. Oracio.
Deus qui beatum
Nicolaum ponti
ficem tuum innumeris de
corasti miraculis tribue
nobis quesumus ut eius
meritis et precibz a gehenne
incendiis liberemur. Per
xpm dnm nostrum. Amen.
De sancto anthonio.

Vox de celo ad an
thonium facta
est quoniam di
micat ecce ego tecum sum et fa

Deus in adiuto
rium meum intende
Domine ad
adiuvandum me festina.

Gloria patri et filio et spi
ritui sancto.
Sicut erat in principio
et nunc et semper et in secula
seculorum.
Amen. Ympnus.
Veni creator spiritus
mentes tuorum
visita imple superna gra
cia que tu creasti pectora.
Memento salutis au
ctor quod nostri quondam cor
poris ex illibata virgine
nascendo formam sumpseris
Maria mater gracie

15 THE MAINZ ANTIPHONER. GERMANY, SECOND HALF OF THE FIFTEENTH CENTURY

With their large folios and rich ornament, choirbooks were highly prized by nineteenth-century collectors. Early in the Museum's history, probably before 1863, a large number of folios were acquired from a single German Antiphoner. One of the leaves had an inscription '149[–]'. Such sets of choirbooks were often produced over a period of years, and the date may represent a local tradition for some event with which the books were associated. The ornament is difficult to assign to a particular centre: it is found over a wide area, but the attribution to the region of Mainz may not be wide of the mark. The text and music are for the Offices of a number of feasts and saints' days. The leaf for Christmas Day has an initial with a Nativity scene, with Joseph shown holding a metal lamp. Feasts for St Benedict perhaps indicate that the choirbook was made for a monastery. St James with his pilgrim's badge and James the Less share a feast – the prominence given to the latter's fuller's staff (used for beating cloth to cleanse it) may point to a cloth-making centre. The undulating acanthus stems issuing from the initial into the margin support a range of flowers, some of them recognizable (roses, columbine, cornflower) but others formulaic, for example the strange petalled flower with a central conical pistil that is the mark of German ornament.

See Elgin Vaasen, 'Die Werkstatt der mainzer Riesenbibel in Würzburg', *Archiv für Geschichte des Buchwesens*, vol. XIII (1973). On problems in studying manuscripts of this kind, see E. König, 'The influence of the invention of printing on the development of German illumination', *Manuscripts in the Fifty Years after the Invention of Printing*, ed. J.B. Trapp (London, 1983)

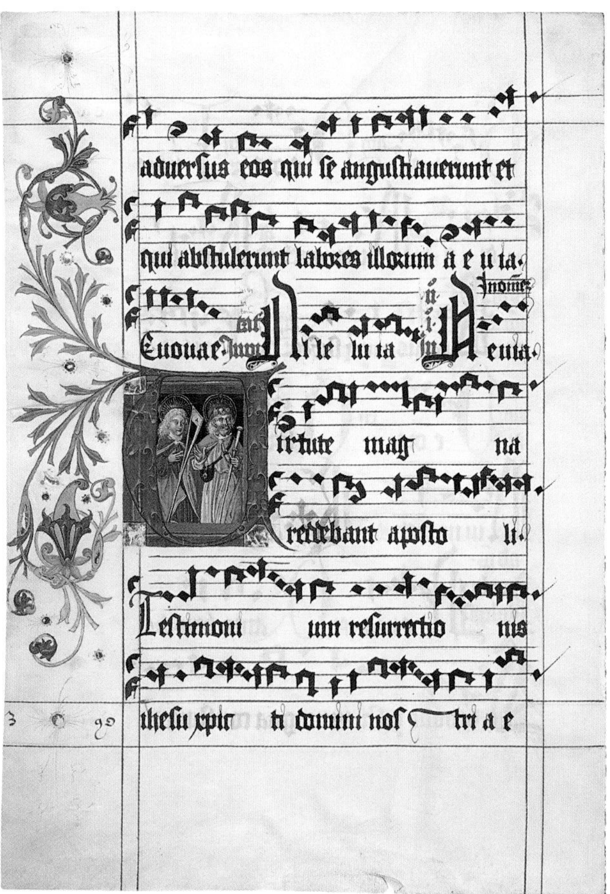

Right: Historiated initial *H* (Nativity).
Left: Leaf with historiated initial *U* (St James of Compostella and St James the Less).

mini habitantia pacis et dominabitur · ps Ds iudicia ·
an Veri tas de ter ra orta est et iustitia de ce
lo prospexit · ps Benedixisti · v Tamquam sponsus ·
Dns
procedens de thalamo suo ·
O di e no
bis ce

16 THE SIMON MARMION BOOK OF HOURS. BRUGES, c.1480

Bruges was at the centre of the commercial heartland of northern Europe, with communities of merchants from Scandinavia, German lands, England, Spain and Italy. Book-producers and miniature-painters in the city supplied clients from all over Europe. This manuscript was evidently done for a notable customer. That it was written in an Italianate, rounded Gothic hand gives no clue as to its first owner, since this script was adopted quite widely in the Bruges book trade from the 1460s for prayerbooks.

It includes the work of four major miniature painters. Miniatures by Simon Marmion are on single leaves; he probably did them in his workshop in Valenciennes, and had them sent to Bruges. They were put into the book to face the texts they served. The opening was then given a unified border decoration by another miniature-painter. The Massacre of the Innocents image for Vespers is thus framed by the work of an illuminator known as the Master of Fitzwilliam 268 (after a manuscript in the Fitzwilliam Museum, Cambridge). Another contributor was William Vrelant, an illuminator whose presence in Bruges is confirmed by archival sources. His style is characterized by drawings with hard outlines and neatly sketched detail within areas of rather undifferentiated colour. This manner is found in so many works that it has been questioned whether Vrelant was an individual or whether the style associated with his name was shared by several illuminators. Vrelant's miniature of St Catherine is on a single leaf, but he also painted the border for the opening, a grey and brown ground with acanthus, fruit and flowers, from which emerge monsters, grotesques, birds and busts of men and women. Another Marmion miniature on a single leaf, the Crucifixion, is part of an opening that has borders by the Master of the Dresden Prayerbook, a distinguished illuminator whose career was centred in Bruges. In the V&A manuscript, he contributed a number of borders in sombre colours yet full of dramatic detail. His portrayal of the human figure in contorted positions shows virtuoso skill.

The collaborative nature of book production in one of northern Europe's main centres of the trade is particularly well illustrated by this manuscript, since the illuminators all had independent careers. In this case, the illustration seems to have begun with Marmion's contribution, imported into Bruges where it was added to. Marmion supplied a set of miniatures on single leaves which included two that were suitable for the Office of the Dead (Christ in Majesty and the Raising of Lazarus). Both were included, but since this left a blank side for one opening, the Fitzwilliam 268 Master was called on to contribute a third scene to make the series run in an uninterrupted fashion. His contribution was a highly original composition, since the conventional illustration had already been provided.

See J.D. Farquhar, 'The Vrelant enigma: is the man the style?', *Quaerendo*, vol. VI (1974); B. Bousmanne, *'Item À Guillaume Wyelant aussi enlumineur': Willem Vrelant* (Turnhout, 1997); B. Brinkmann, *Die flämische Buchmalerei am Ende des Burgunderreichs: Der Meister des Dresdener Gebetbuchs und die Miniaturistens seiner Zeit*, 2 vols (Turnhout, 1997); see also B. Brinkmann's contribution to *Margaret of York, Simon Marmion, and The Visions of Tondal*, ed. T. Kren (Malibu, 1992)

Above: f.103v Vespers with the Massacre of the Innocents.

Top right: f.15v-16 Prayer to St Catherine with the martyrdom of the saint.
Bottom right: ff.18v-19 Hours of the Cross with the Crucifixion.

Commemoracio de scā
katherina
Gaude uir
go kathe
rina. qua
doctores
lex diuina
triuit ab erroribus
Gaude pro qua tenebro
sus. carcer fuit luminosus
flagrans ex odoribus.
Gaude conuertens regi
nam. cernens rotarū rui
nam. plebis i discrimine.
Gaude tu que flagella
ris. et post preces decolla

Incipit officium de scā
cruce. Ad matutinas:
Domine
labia me
a aperies
Et os me
um an
nuntia
bit laudem tuam Deus
in adiutorium meū in
tende. Domine ad adiu
uandum me festina. Glo
ria patri et filio: et spiri
tui sancto. Sicut erat
in principio et nunc; et
semper: et in secula secu

17 BOOK OF HOURS. WRITTEN IN THE RHINELAND AND ILLUMINATED IN FLANDERS, *c.*1480

In German-speaking lands, Books of Hours were not the standard aid to personal devotions that they were in France, the Netherlands or England – prayerbooks of other kinds were preferred. This Book of Hours is remarkable for being written in German, in a dialect spoken in the region between Strasbourg and Karlsruhe on the Rhine, for a calendar where Trier saints are given pride of place, and for the form of devotions defined as the Use of Basel. Such variety contrasts with the standardized products of the French and Netherlandish book trades. The ornament and miniatures belong to a totally different area – Flanders. The miniatures are painted in a restricted range of colours, while the clumsy perspective, employing tall thin pillars in the foreground, supporting arcades or vaulted ceilings, attempts to create an effect of recession. Facial features are drawn with sharp black lines. The style recalls that of emulators of the Master of Margaret of York school in Bruges, but there are also resemblances to manuscripts from the county of Hainaut.

The obvious question is whether a miniature painter from Flanders was active in the Upper Rhineland area, or whether the manuscript was sent to Flanders for decoration. The latter solution seems more likely. The miniatures are not well integrated with the text, so that the writing and the illumination seem to have been two independent campaigns. Parts of the text left unilluminated received initials characteristic of work in the Upper Rhineland. However keen the connoisseur may be to discover a local school with consistent, identifiable characteristics, this does not always accord well either with the notion of collaborative work by travelling illuminators, or the fact that books were produced over a period of time and sent to different centres for the various stages of production.

This manuscript was owned by one Mathias Eberhart in the sixteenth century, possibly identifiable as Mathis Bernhart, who was Master of Works of Colmar Cathedral. He is referred to in archival sources of 1567 and the 1570s. In any case, Mathias gave the book to his sister Rebecca Sigerstein (d.1610), who was prioress of the convent of Unterlinden in Colmar.

See *Les dominicaines d'Unterlinden*, 2 vols (Paris and Colmar, 2000)

ff.53v-54 Miniature of the owner, with Vespers and the Purification opposite.

Herre vergib dyne knechten ir sunde: want wir mogen dir nit gefallen mit unseren deden: darumb behalde uns von der muder unsers heren ihu cristi dyns sones: der da zukunfftich ist zu ortelen die lebendigē unde die doden: Amen.

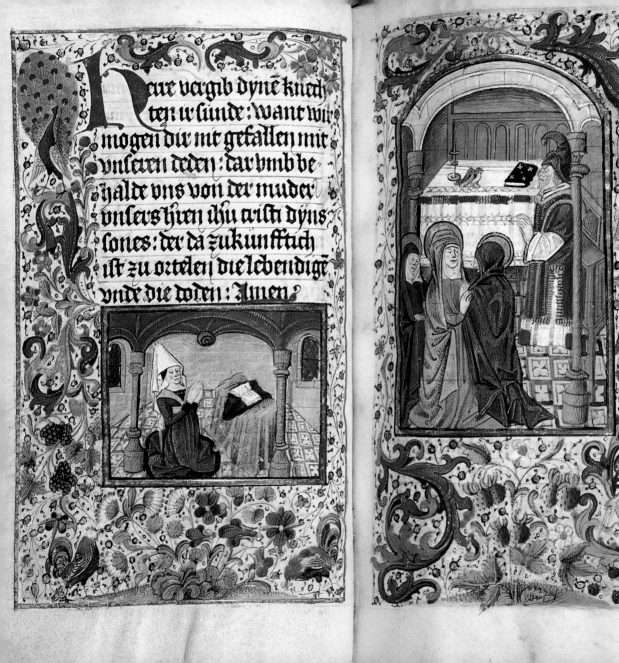

18 Leaf from the Giltlingen Missal. Augsburg, *c.*1485–89

Johann von Giltlingen was abbot of the rich monastery of Saints Afra and Ulrich in Augsburg between 1482 and 1496. Among the brethren were Leonard Wagner of Schwabmenchigen, a scribe, and Conrad Wagner of Ellingen (apparently not a close relation), an illuminator. The chronicle of the abbey describes their work. Conrad Wagner is referred to as '*bonus illuminista*' and as '*diversis artibus . . . instructus*' ('a good illuminator', 'skilful in many arts'). He was said to have produced several books, namely 'Breviaries, Diurnals and the Missal of Lord Johann of Giltlingen, abbot'.

The Missal was a sumptuous manuscript, clearly not produced under undue constraints of time and expense. The border has a ground of burnished gold on which are conventional sprays of acanthus and stylized flowers in rich blues, reds, ochres and greens. The multicoloured moulded frame around the marginal ornament and the historiated initial are characteristic of German illumination, though they are usually confined to the initial or miniature. The initial contains a scene of the Adoration of the Magi, one of them black and fashionably dressed (a short coat held in at the waist and tights) rather than robed. In the lower margin are scenes of the Baptism of Christ and the Wedding at Cana. It seems significant that another manuscript produced at the abbey, a Psalter, was sent to the city in 1494–95 for illumination by a lay illuminator, Georg Beck, either because more painterly qualities were required (a leaf from this Psalter is in the V&A, and it contains what is virtually a small panel painting) or because other aspects of ornament prevented Wagner from undertaking the work. The chronicle says that Conrad Wagner '*illuminavit et corporavit [libros]*' ('he illuminated and gave figures to books'), but perhaps he confined himself to small-scale work. The sources for his images can be found among compositions current in the Augsburg book trade; he is known to have copied an image of a Pentecost scene published by Günther Zainer in 1473, but he also modelled compositions on the prints of Martin Schongauer, which were among the most widely distributed sources of images at this time.

Leaves from the Giltlingen Missal are in several other collections, widely distributed by the nineteenth-century art trade. Some include the dates 1485 and 1489 – a testimony to the time it took to finish this prestige work.

See James Marrow, 'Two newly identified leaves from the Missal of Johannes von Giltlingen: notes on late fifteenth-century manuscript illumination in Augsburg', *Anzeiger des Germanischen Nationalmuseums* (1984), pp. 27–31; W.M. Voelkle and R.S. Wieck, *The Bernard H. Breslauer Collection of Manuscript Illuminations* (New York, 1992)

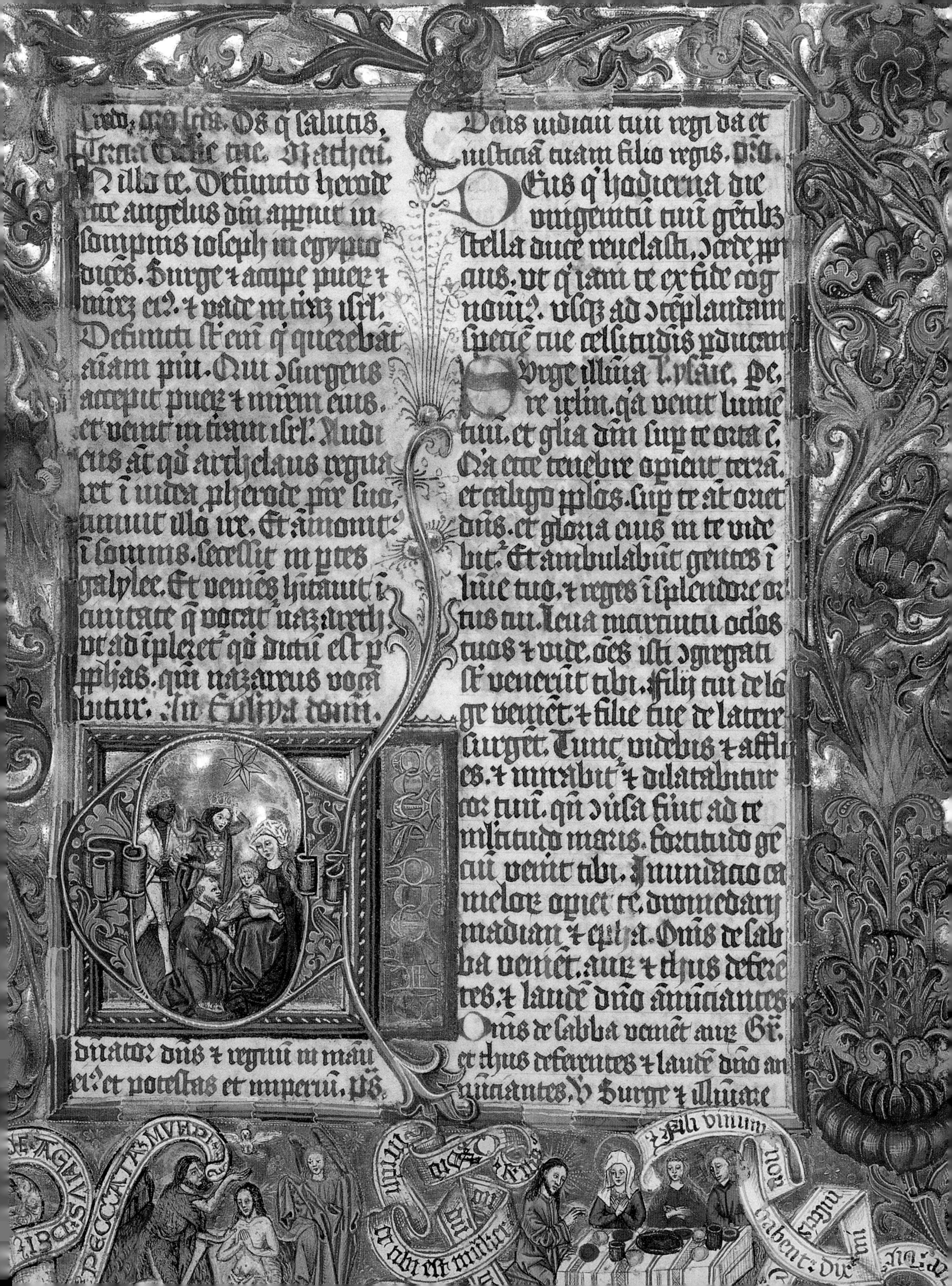

[...] Os q̄ salutis, terra Galilee tue. Mathei. In illo te. Defuncto herode ecce angelus dñi apparuit in sompnis ioseph in egypto dicẽs. Surge et accipe puerũ et matrẽ eius et vade in terrã isrl. Defuncti sũt enĩ q̄ querebãt aĩam pueri. Qui surgens accepit puerũ et matrem eius. et venit in terram isrl. Audiens aũt q̄ archelaus regnaret ĩ iudea p herode pre suo. timuit illo ire. Et amonit? i sompnis. secessit in ptes galylee. Et veniẽs habitavit ĩ civitate q̄ vocat nazareth. ut adimpleret qd dictũ est p pphas. qm nazareus vocabitur. In Epiphania domini.

[E] ... dnator dñs et regnũ in manu eius et potestas et imperiũ. Ps.

Deus iudicium tuum regi da et iusticiã tuam filio regis. Or.

Deus q̄ hodierna die unigenitũ tuũ gẽtibus stella duce revelasti, concede propitius, ut q̄ iam te ex fide cognovim?, usq3 ad contemplandam speciẽ tue celsitudinis pducamur. Surge illuminare. Ysaie. Lc.

Surge illumina ierlm. q̄a venit lumẽ tuũ. et glia dñi sup te orta ẽ. Q̄a ecce tenebre opient terrã. et caligo pplos. sup te aũt orietur dñs. et gloria eius in te videbit. Et ambulabũt gentes ĩ lumĩe tuo. et reges ĩ splendore ortus tui. Leva in circuitu oc'los tuos et vide. oẽs isti cõgregati sũt venerũt tibi. Filii tui de longe venĩet. et filie tue de latere surgẽt. Tunc videbis et afflues. et mirabit et dilatabitur cor tuũ. qñ conversa fuit ad te multitudo maris. fortitudo gentiũ venit tibi. Inundatio camelorũ operiet te. dromedarii madian et epha. Oms de saba venĩet. aurũ et thus deferentes. et laudẽ dño annũciantes. Oms de sabba venĩet aurũ Gr. et thus deferentes et laudẽ dño annunciantes. V Surge et illuminare

19 The Sanvito Cicero of 1495 and a printed emulator: Julius Caesar Commentarorium de bello Gallico Libri VIII (Venice: heirs of Aldus Manutius, 1519)

In the 1490s the scribe Bartolomeo Sanvito produced a series of manuscripts in a small format for clients in Rome. Most were texts of Cicero. This manuscript, dated 1495, was made for a cardinal, Raffaello Riario (1451–1521), whose arms appear on the first page. The ornament, of characteristic classical motifs, has the coloured shading that makes it appear in relief. This was a technique perfected by Sanvito himself, who is now considered to have been an illuminator as well as a scribe.

The V&A manuscript was of a kind that provided the model for one of the most successful publishing enterprises of the Renaissance, the Aldine classics. These were a series of texts in Latin and Greek produced by the Venetian publisher Aldus Manutius. In their small format and (for the Latin texts) their page design and typography, they appear to have copied the exquisite small manuscripts that were Bartolomeo Sanvito's speciality. Sanvito has been proposed as the designer of the italic printing font that Aldus had made for his press, first used in 1501. The link may, however, have been an indirect one. Aldus's press was a meeting place of contemporary scholars – his products had the aura of being sanctioned by the best minds of the day, and such manuscripts as the V&A Cicero were perhaps to be found in their libraries. Sanvito was certainly known by people in the circle of Aldus. Though devoid of the kind of archaeological ornament that occurs in Sanvito's manuscripts (but still capable of being embellished and made usable by illuminated initials and other features), Aldus's pocket editions were a spectacular success throughout Europe. They satisfied the demands of a generation hungry for texts of recently rediscovered Greek and Roman writers in their original languages. The books continued to be printed after the death of Aldus in 1515. In such cases, printing was making widely available what had previously been commissioned by rich connoisseurs and scholars.

See M. Lowry, *The World of Aldus Manutius: Business and Scholarship in Renaissance Venice* (Oxford, 1979); Martin Davis, *Aldus Manutius: Publisher and Printer of the Renaissance* (London, 1995); J.J.G. Alexander and A.C. de la Mare, *Italian Manuscripts in the Library of Major J.R. Abbey* (London, 1969), pp. 104 ff.

Top: Caesar pp.64v–65.
Bottom: Cicero ff.82v–83.

C. IVLII CAESARIS COMMENTARIORVM DE BELLO GALLICO LIBER SEXTVS.

MVLTIS DE causis Cæsar maiorē Galliæ motum expectās per M. Sylanum. C. Antistium reginū T. Sextium legatos delectum habere instituit. Simul ab Cn. Pompeio proconsule petit, quoniam ipse ad urbem cum imperio reipub. causa maneret, quos ex cisalpina Gallia consulis sacramento rogauisset ad signa conuenire, & ad se proficisci iuberet, magni interesse etiam in reliquum tempus, ad opinionem Galliæ existimans, tantas uideri Italiæ facultates, ut siquid esset in bello detrimenti acceptum, non modo id breui tempore sarciri, sed etiam maioribus adaugeri copijs posset, quod cum Pompeius, & reipub. & amicitiæ tribuisset, celeriter confecto per suos delectu tribus ante exactam hyemem, & constitutis, & adductis legionibus, duplicatoq; earum cohortium numero, quas cum Q. Titurio amiserat, & celeritate, et copijs docuit, qd populi Romani disciplina, atq; opes possent. Interfecto Induciomaro, ut docuimus, ad eius propinquos à Treueris imperiū defertur. Illi finitimos, atq; Germanos solicitare, & pecuniam polliceri non desistunt, cum ab proximus impetrare non possent, ulteriores tentant, inuētis nonnullis ciuitatibus iureiurando inter se cōfirmant, obsidibusq; de pecunia cauent. Ambiorigem sibi societate, et fœdere adiungunt. Quibus

rebus cognitis

rebus cognitis Cæsar, cum undiq; bellum parari uideret, Neruios, Aduaticos, ac Menapios, adiunctis cisrhenanis omnibus Germanis esse in armis. Senōnes ad imperatum non uenire, et cum Carnutibus, finitimisq; ciuitatibus consilia communicare, à Treueris Germanos crebis legationibus solicitari, maturius sibi de Bello cogitandum putauit. Itaq; non dum hyeme confecta, proximis quatuor legionibus coactis, de improuiso in fines Neruiorum contendit, et prius, q̄ illi aut conuenire, aut profugere possent, magno pecoris, atq; hominū numero capto, atq; ea præda militibus concessa, uastatisq; agris, in deditionem uenire, atq; obsides sibi dare coegit. Eo celeriter confecto negocio rursus legiones in hyberna reduxit. Consilio Galliæ primo uere (ut instituerat) indicto, cum reliq̄ præter Senōnes, Carnutes, Treurosq; uenissent, initium belli, ac defectionis hoc esse arbitratus, ut omnia postponere uideretur, cōciliū in Lutetiam Parisiorum transfert. (Confines erant hi Senonibus, ciuitatemq; patrum memoria coniunxerant, sed ab hoc consilio abfuisse existimabātur.) Hac re pro suggestu pronuntiata, eodem die cum legionibus in Senōnes proficiscitur, magnisq; itineribus eò p̄uenit. Cognito eius aduentu Acco, qui princeps eius consilij fuerat: iubet in oppida multitudinem conuenire, Conantibus, prius q̄ id effici posset, adesse Romanos nuntiatur: necessario sententia desistunt, legatosq; deprecandi causa ad Cæsarem mittunt, Adeunt per Heduos, quorum antiquitus erat in fide ciuitas, libēter Cæsar petentibus Heduis, dat ueniam, excusationemq; accipit, quod æstiuum tempus instantis belli, nō quæstionis esse arbitra

in latinum conuertimus.

COMPARATIO DVORVM VTILIVM INTER SE.

SEd utilitatum comparatio (quoniam hic locus erat quartus a Panetio prætermissus) sæpe est necessaria. Nam & corporis comoda cū externis: & externa cum corporis: & ipsa inter se corporis: & externa cū externis comparari solent. Cum externis corporis hoc modo comparantur: ualere ut malis q̄ diues esse. Cum corporis externa hoc modo: diues esse potius q̄ maximis corporis uiribus. Ipsa inter se corporis comparantur sic: ut bona ualitudo uoluptati anteponatur: uires celeritati. Externorum aūt: ut gloria diuitijs: uectigalia urbana rusticis. Ex quo genere comparationis illud est Catonis senis. A quo cū quæreretur quid maxime in re familiari expediret: respondit, bene pascere. Quid secundū? satis bene pascere. Quid tertiū? bene uestire. Quid quartū? arare. Et cū ille q quæsierat dixisset: quid fœnerari. Tum Cato: quid hoiem, inquit, occidere? Ex quo & multis

Quid in re familiari expediat.

Catonis sententia

alijs intelligi debet utilitatū comparationes solere fieri: recteq; hoc adiunctum esse quartū exquirendorum officiorum genus. Sed toto hoc de genere de quærenda, de collocanda pecunia, & de utenda: comodius a quibusdā optimis uiris ad medium ianuæ sedentibus q̄ ab ullis philosophis ulla in schola disputatur. Sunt at ea cognoscenda. Pertinent enim ad utilitatem: de qua hoc libro disputatū est. Reliqua deinceps persequemur.

M. T. C. OFFICIORVM LIBER. III.

PSCIPIONEM. M. FILI EVM QVI PRIMVM APHRIcanus appellatus est dicere solitū scripsit Cato: qui fuit fere eius æqualis:

Aphricanus.

Cato

20 Book of Hours. Paris, *c.*1500

This Book of Hours represents a new design: the writing is in a very small *bâtarde* script ('bastard' script, see p. 14) and is densely arranged in two columns on the page; small miniatures are integrated into the columns. The Penitential Psalms have a full-page miniature. Within a simple architectural frame, Christ sits in judgement at the end of time; to his right the Virgin and female saints praying; to his left John the Baptist and male saints. In the lower register the dead emerge from graves and from a lake, and are led either to Hell (on the right) or referred to Heaven. This image gained wide currency as a woodcut in the Hours printed in 1498 by Pigouchet for the bookseller Simon Vostre.

The images used for the printed Hours of Pigouchet are attributable to the illuminator of a small prayerbook made for Anne de Bretagne, the Master of the Très Petites Heures d'Anne de Bretagne. He worked in various media, providing woodcuts for printers but also designs for tapestries and stained glass (he was once known as the Master of the Chasse à la Licorne, from the tapestry of this name). The V&A manuscript is similar to the work of this artist – the compositions and use of colour in the miniatures are comparable to those in the Très Petites Heures, though the border ornament is quite different. The finish to faces and other parts of the body suggest some differences in the preparation of pigments, while the use of brushed-gold highlights seems less systematic in the Anne de Bretagne manuscript.

See Geneviève Souchal, 'Un grand peintre français de la fin du XVe siècle: le Maître de la Chasse à la Licorne', *Revue de L'Art*, no. 22 (1973), pp. 22–49; François Avril and Nicole Reynaud, *Les Manuscrits à peintures en France, 1440–1520* (Paris, 1994); on the Master of the Chasse à la Licorne, see Sterling, 1987–90, vol. II

Right: ff.19v–20 f.19v Penitential Psalms with miniature of Christ in Judgement.
Above: Pigouchet, Book of Hours printed for Simon Vostre, 1498.

Domine ne in furore
tuo arguas me: ne-
que in ira tua corri-
pias me.
Miserere mei domine quoniam
infirmus sum: sana me
domine quoniam conturba-
ta sunt ossa mea.
Et anima mea turbata est
valde: sed tu domine usquequo.
Convertere domine et eripe
animam meam: salvum me
fac propter misericordiam tuam.
Quoniam non est in morte
qui memor sit tui: in inferno
autem quis confitebitur tibi.
Laboravi in gemitu meo la-
vabo per singulas noctes lectum
meum: lacrimis meis stratum
meum rigabo.
Turbatus est a furore oculus
meus: inveteravi inter omnes
inimicos meos.
Discedite a me omnes qui
operamini iniquitatem: quoniam
exaudivit dominus vocem fletus mei.
Exaudivit dominus de-
precationem meam: dominus
orationem meam suscepit.
Erubescant et conturbentur
vehementer omnes inimici
mei: convertantur et erubescant valde velociter. Gloria.
Beati quorum remisse
sunt iniquitates: et
quorum tecta sunt peccata.
Beatus vir cui non imputa-
vit dominus peccatum:
nec est in spiritu eius dolus.
Quoniam tacui inveterave-
runt ossa mea: dum
clamarem tota die.
Quoniam die ac nocte gra-
vata est super me manus
tua: conversus sum in erum-
na mea: dum configitur
spina.

Delictum meum cognitum
tibi feci: et iniustitiam meam
non abscondi.
Dixi confitebor adversum me
iniustitiam meam domino: et
tu remisisti impietatem peccati mei.
Pro hac orabit ad te omnis sanc-
tus: in tempore oportuno.
Verumtamen in diluvio aquarum multarum: ad eum non
approximabunt.
Tu es refugium meum a
tribulatione que circumdedit
me: exultatio mea erue me
a circumdantibus me.
Intellectum tibi dabo et in-
struam te in via hac qua gra-
dieris: firmabo super te oculos
meos.
Nolite fieri sicut equus et
mulus: quibus non est intellectus.
In chamo et freno maxillas
eorum constringe: qui non
approximant ad te.
Multa flagella peccatoris:
sperantem autem in domino
misericordia circumdabit.
Letamini in domino et
exultate iusti: et gloriamini
omnes recti corde. Gloria patri.
Domine ne in furore
tuo arguas me: neque
in ira tua corripias me.
Quoniam sagitte tue infi-
xe sunt michi: et confirmasti
super me manum tuam.
Non est sanitas in carne
mea a facie ire tue: non est
pax ossibus meis a facie
peccatorum meorum.
Quoniam iniquitates
mee supergresse sunt caput
meum: et sicut onus grave
gravate sunt super me.
Putruerunt et corrupte
sunt cicatrices mee a facie
insipientie mee.

Incipit offitium beate marie virginis secundum curiam romanã
Ad matutinum. Versus

Domine la-
bia mea ape-
ries. R. Et os
meum annũ-
tiabit laudẽ
tuam. V.

Deus in adiutorium meum intende
Domine ad adiuvandum me festina
Gloria patri et filio et spiritui sancto
Sicut erat in principio et nunc et semp[er]
et in secula seculorum amen. Alleluia
Et dicatur a pascha resurrectionis us-
que ad septuagesimam. et a septuage

21 THE SERRISTORI HOURS. FLORENCE, *c.*1510

Both in format and ornament, this Book of Hours is characteristic of luxury prayerbooks produced in Florence in the early sixteenth century. The binding, contemporary with the manuscript, has gold-tooled ornament with arabesque and knotwork motifs. As regards the illumination, the scrolled acanthus on rich grounds of green, blue or red is interspersed with medallions bearing either pictures of saints or devices of the Serristori family (a pair of wings and the motto '*DII BENE VERTANT*'; a pair of clasping hands in front of a triangular point emitting gold rays). The version of the family's arms lacks the Medici device granted by Pope Leo X in 1515, which provides an element of dating.

The medallion in the left margin shows Diomedes and the palladium, a version of a celebrated gem owned by the Medici family (Vespasiano da Bisticci referred to it, evidence of its currency in the book trade). That on the right shows a warrior with a Victory figurine, representing Rome (the warrior may be Apollo – the quiver of arrows was one of his marks). The latter is flanked vertically by two small red cameos; the device of a cherub astride a cock on one corresponds to the supporters of the Serristori arms. The leafy acanthus initials throughout the manuscript were widely used in Italy for liturgical and devotional books in the last quarter of the fifteenth century and after. Though rich in effect, the colouring depends on a restricted number of pigments – red, blue, green and gold – for its impact.

The main miniatures are all on single leaves, which receive the same illuminated ornament as the body of the book. They have been attributed to Mariano del Buono di Jacopo, with contributions from Monte di Giovanni for the St Jerome miniature. Mariano died in 1504, but his style was maintained after this date, as was that of the ornament with which it was associated.

See Annarosa Garzelli, *Miniatura fiorentina del rinascimento, 1440–1525* ([Florence], 1985); for similar manuscripts, L.M.J. Delaissé *et al.*, *The James A. de Rothschild Collection at Waddesdon Manor: Illuminated Manuscripts* (National Trust, 1977)

Left: ff.6v–7 End of calendar and beginning of the Office of the Virgin, with historiated initial *D* (Nativity).

Above: ff.57v–58 Office of the Dead, with three living and three dead kings and the hermit Macarius; opposite historiated initial *O* (the raising of Lazarus).

22 THE LEUVILLE EPISTLES. TOURS(?), *c.*1520–1530

In the face of a rising tide of printed works, illumination survived (where it was not absorbed as a menial task in the book trade) as a de luxe profession. This small manuscript copy of the Epistles is one of a group of more than sixteen that have been described as products of the '1520s Hours workshop'. They have a common format and design: all are on fine, supple parchment, and were written in Roman and italic scripts that gave perfected versions of printed typefaces. The ornament is an extravagant French version of Italian styles, of a kind introduced into France when manuscripts illuminated by Giovanni Todeschino came to Tours with the library of Frederick III of Naples after he was banished from the Italian kingdom in 1501. The painting is characterized by dramatic poses and elongated contrapposto positions for figures, and naturalistic landscapes with idealized and finely reproduced castles and townscapes in the distance. These features reflect what is known as the 'Antwerp Mannerist' style, whose influence in France has been linked to the presence in Paris of Godefroy le Batave.

This manuscript contains the work of two illuminators. The miniatures for the Prologue and the beginning of the Pauline Epistles (ff.1v, 7v) are by a hand known as the Claude of France Master, who used compositions and ornament also found in manuscripts illuminated by Jean Bourdichon and Jean Poyet, both active in the Tours region. The image of St Peter (f.168v) has been attributed to the miniaturist of a Book of Hours made for Jean de Mauléon, made Bishop of St Bertrand de Comminges in 1519. The miniatures of St John and St Jude may be by the Master of the Doheny Hours, a close follower.

The arms on the delicately enamelled clasps of the binding identify the Leuville family as the original owners. The best candidate is Jean Olivier (d.1542), an accomplished Latinist who was elected Bishop of Angers in 1532, though his brother, François Olivier de Leuville (1505–65), a senior government minister who became chancellor in 1545, is also a possibility.

See Myra D. Orth, 'French Renaissance manuscripts: the 1520s Hours Workshop and the Master of the Getty Epistles', *The J. Paul Getty Museum Journal*, vol. XVI (1988), pp. 33–60; M. Baker and B. Richardson, eds, *A Grand Design: The Art of the Victoria and Albert Museum* (London, 1997)

Opposite: f.1v St Jerome in the wilderness.

INCI
bus no
di plen
apostol
ecclesia
factum
scentis
bus pra
orienti
ras exc
proph
Moisi:
legeba
ctrina
compr

23 A CHARTER ILLUMINATED BY LUCAS HORENBOUT. LONDON, 1524

These letters patent, dated 28 April 1524, record the grant to one Thomas Forster of property in Bishopsgate, London. The document at once raises a host of problems. The portrait of the king can, on the basis of comparison with the famous miniature of Henry VIII in the Fitzwilliam Museum, be confidently attributed to Lucas Horenbout, an illuminator from the 'Ghent–Bruges' school (see no. 24) who came to England and found employment with Henry VIII's court. The Fitzwilliam miniature is dated 1525–26. It has been assumed that Lucas was called to England to serve at the royal court; the first payments to him in royal archives are dated September 1525.

Miniature portraits were to become one of the glories

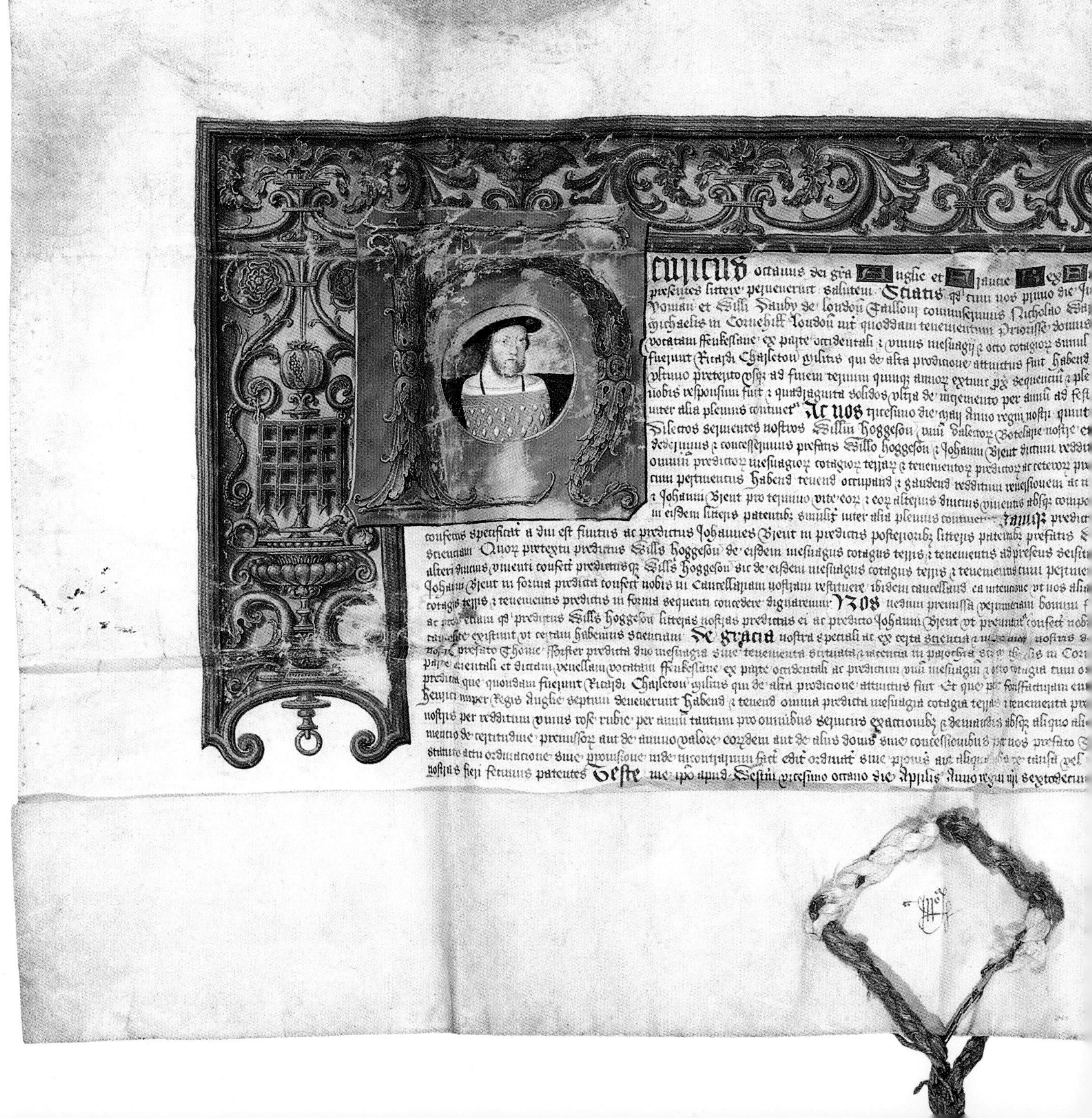

of English painting, cherished by a circle of courtiers. This makes it odd that the first appearance of the famous image of Henry VIII should be in a document that had nothing to do with courtiers and was remote from the elite world in which miniature painting developed. Even if the portrait was added after 1524, which is possible, the appearance of this highly sophisticated 'Ghent–Bruges' ornament on a totally conventional title deed of 1524 is surprising – this was to be a courtly art, not one that was adopted in business circles.

The ornament on the letters patent shows the arrival in England of the elaborate 'Ghent–Bruges' version of Italian Renaissance ornament, probably already known through a variety of media including manuscripts illuminated abroad and printed books. Florentine printers and, following them, printers in German lands had adapted for title pages and borders the candelabra, leafy masks, dolphin heads and cherub faces that were common currency in Italy. Hans Baldung Grien's title pages, for instance, show an ornamental vocabulary echoed in ornament used by Simon Bening in such works as the Golf Hours in the British Library. Painters such as Bening's fellow-townsman Lancelot Blondeel in Bruges in the 1520s developed it with astonishing enthusiasm. The 1524 document includes royal devices (the portcullis of the Beaufort family inherited from Henry VII's mother; the Tudor rose; the pomegranate of Catherine of Aragon, Henry VIII's first wife) on a mottled pink ground. The initial *H* that shelters the portrait imitates Italian initials; the bracelets of cameo-portraits on the stem and bowl are a feature that can be traced there from the last quarter of the fifteenth century.

See Lorne Campbell and Susan Foister, 'Gerard, Lucas and Susannah Horenbout', *Burlington Magazine*, vol. CXVIII, no. 1003 (1986), pp. 719–27; Janet Backhouse, 'Illuminated manuscripts and the early development of the portrait miniature', *Early Tudor England: Proceedings of the 1987 Harlaxton Symposium*, ed. Daniel Williams (1989); Katherine Coombs, *The Portrait Miniature in England* (V&A, 1998)

24 A Book of Hours illuminated by Simon Bening. Bruges, early sixteenth century

Simon Bening was a major figure in what is known as the 'Ghent–Bruges' school, a term still used although it is now known that works in this style were also produced in other cities. A totally new style of book decoration emerged in around 1480 (continuing until the 1560s), characterized by miniatures with realistically depicted figures in spacious landscapes or intimate interiors (the subtle colouring and carefully built-up pigments contrast with styles like that associated with Vrelant). Marginal ornament is still arresting in its naturalism – carefully portrayed flowers, including pinks, roses, columbines, pansies, irises and pea-flowers, are scattered on a brushed gold ground so as to cast a shadow. They are accompanied by fruits, insects and birds, some of which play *trompe-l'oeil* tricks by disregarding the boundaries of the page, whether threaded through it, for example, or strolling across it, as one fly irreverently does.

Realistic portrayal of flowers can be traced back in both French and Italian illuminated manuscripts to the fourteenth century. Fifteenth-century manuscripts such as the Margaret of Orléans Hours have wonderfully observed irises set in a conventional border ornament of stylized acanthus. The realism of the 'Ghent–Bruges' school appears to antedate the nature studies of artists such as Dürer, but it is confined to decorative purposes. The 'Ghent–Bruges' border ornament became a standard for the sixteenth century, and was widely imitated in less expert forms in books, documents and other media.

This fragmentary Book of Hours contains only the Penitential Psalms, Office of the Dead and suffrages to saints. It may have been split off from other texts in the seventeenth century, when it was given a splendid gold-tooled binding and expensive decorated endpapers. The image of David in Penitence (he is shown acknowledging his adultery with Bathsheba and the murder of her husband) includes Romanesque architectural detail and a Flemish palace. The classical candelabrum with cornucopia and dragons shows the absorption of designs from Renaissance Italy. The funeral service and procession is an identical composition to the Rothschild Hours (until recently in Vienna), attributed to Gerard Horenbout, but here the palette is darker, the carnation for the faces more muddy, and the range of colour more restricted.

See: the facsimile, *Simon Bening: Le livre d'heures aux fleurs Das Blumen-Stundenbuch*, commentary by Bodo Brinkmann and Eberhard Köenig (Lucerne, 1991); Judith Testa, *The Beatty Rosarium: A Manuscript with Miniatures by Simon Bening* (Doornspijk, 1986); Thomas Kren, 'Landscape as leitmotif: a reintegrated Book of Hours illuminated by Simon Bening', *Illuminating the Book: Makers and Interpreters: Essays in Honour of Janet Backhouse*, ed. M.P. Brown and S. McKendrick (London, 1998); for the Horenbout manuscript, see Ernst Trenkler, *Rothschild-Gebetbuch: Vollständige Faksimile* (Graz, 1979)

Top: ff.2v–3 Penitential Psalms with David in penitence; opposite, in the border, David in front of a mounted king and his army, bearing the head of Goliath on a sword.

Bottom: ff.21v–22 Office of the Dead: funeral service, in front of a furnished altar; opposite, within a border, a funeral procession.

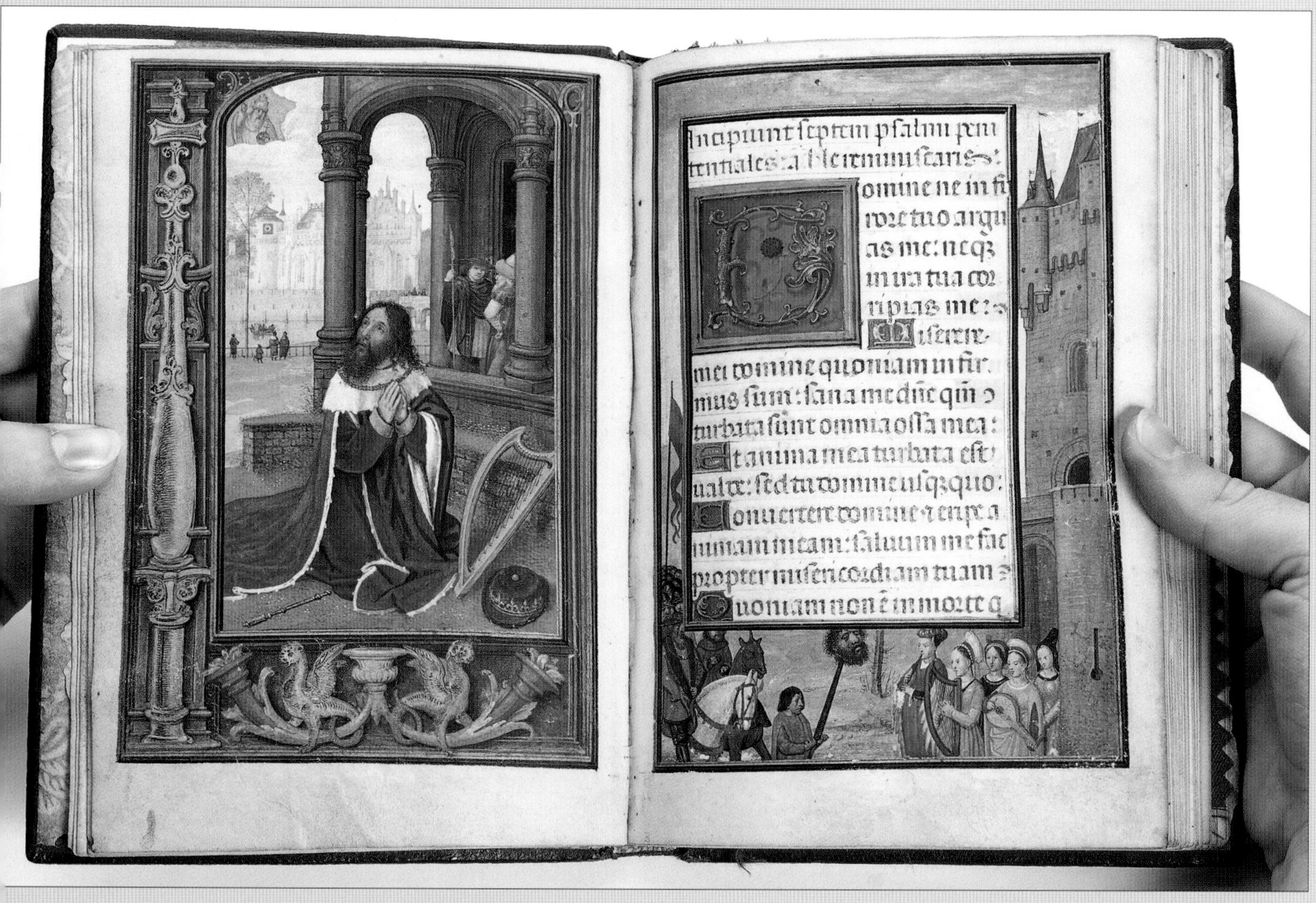
Incipiunt septem psalmi peni
tentiales: a[n]t[iphona] Ne reminiscaris
Domine ne in fu
rore tuo argu
as me: neq[ue]
in ira tua cor
ripias me:
Miserere
mei domine quoniam infir
mus sum: sana me d[omi]ne q[uonia]m
turbata sunt omnia ossa mea:
Et anima mea turbata est
valde: sed tu domine usq[ue]quo:
Convertere domine et eripe a
nimam meam: salvum me fac
propter misericordiam tuam
Quoniam non est in morte q

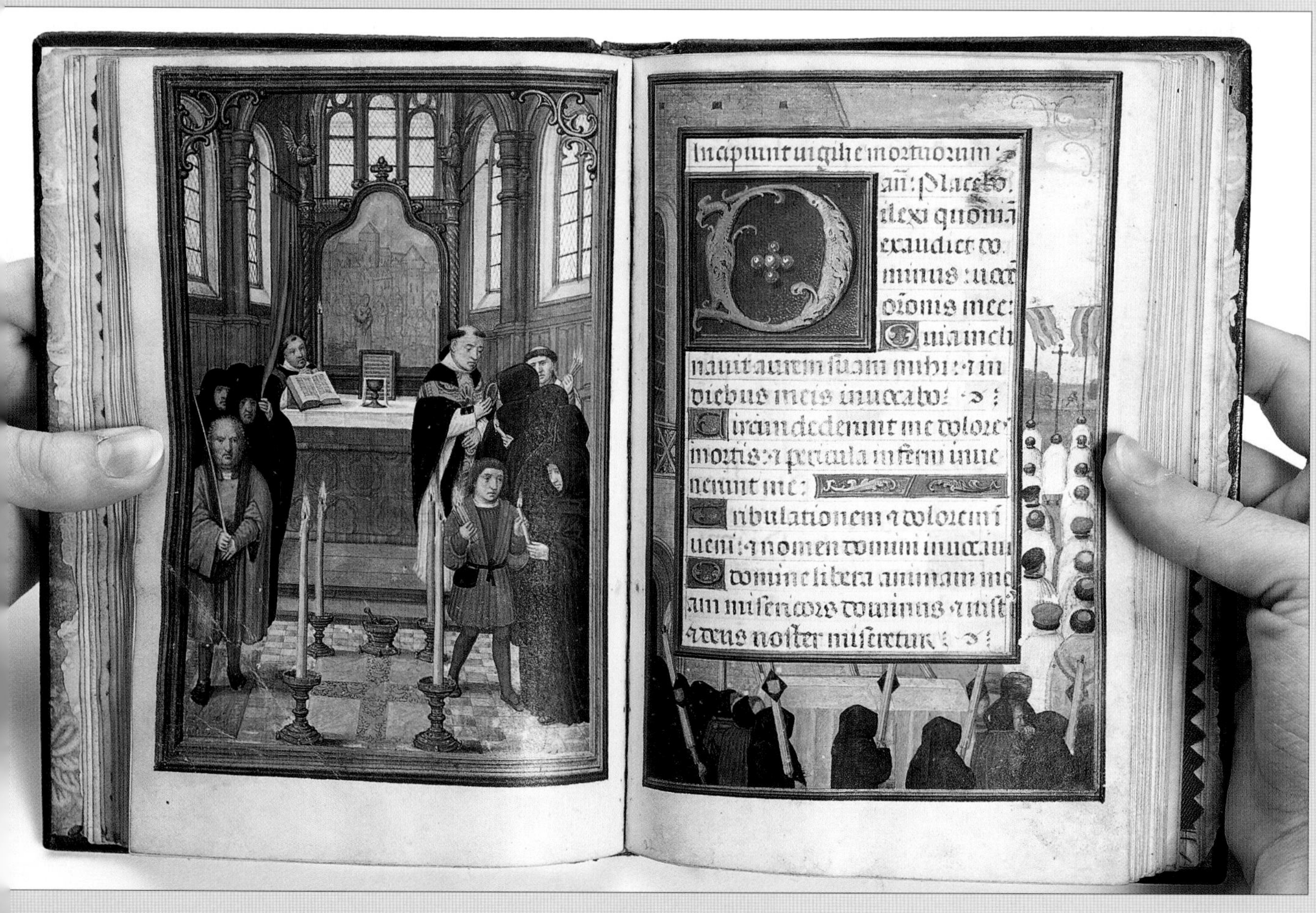
Incipiunt vigilie mortuorum:
a[n]t[iphona] Placebo.
Dilexi quoniam
exaudiet do
minus: voce[m]
orationis mee:
Quia incli
navit aurem suam mihi: et in
diebus meis invocabo:
Circumdederunt me dolores
mortis: et pericula inferni inve
nerunt me:
Tribulationem et dolorem in
veni: et nomen domini invocavi
O domine libera animam me
am misericors dominus et iust
et deus noster miseretur:

25 The Armagnac Manuscript of the Trial and Rehabilitation of Joan of Arc. Rouen, 1530s

Joan of Arc was burnt by the English authorities in Rouen in May, 1431. The French king, Charles VII, who regained Paris in 1436 and Rouen in 1450, instituted a commission to examine her conviction, but its report in 1452 did not lead to action. In 1455 the pope ordered Jean Jouvenal des Ursins, Archbishop of Rheims, to investigate the case; in 1456 the latter declared that Joan had been falsely convicted and executed, thus clearing her name of treachery and witchcraft.

In the late fifteenth century Joan was gradually assimilated to the rank of heroine: Martin Le Franc compared her to Judith, who killed the tyrant Holofernes to save her people, and by the next century she was listed among the ranks of worthy women whose virtues ought to be emulated.

This manuscript was prepared for Diane de Poitiers (1499–1566). It contains two prefaces to her that refer to her 'majesty', possibly suggesting that she was by that time mistress of the Dauphin (i.e. winter of 1538–39; the Dauphin was to become Henri II in 1547). Diane's husband, Louis de Brézé, had died in 1531; his tomb in Rouen Cathedral, constructed by Diane, was one of the first Renaissance monuments of this kind in France (the palaces of Anet and Chenonceau by the famous Philibert de l'Orme were to be further examples of her passion for Italian art). The ornament on the full-page image is in a Renaissance style (cherubs at play within an arcaded gallery set into an classical gateway), but the images themselves are, perhaps intentionally, in a rather old-fashioned manner, with simple areas of contrasting colour and roughly drawn faces. The miniatures illustrate Joan's condemnation and episodes in the process of the revision: the king (presumably Henry VI) presiding over the condemnation; Charles VII giving a message to the lawyer Paul du Pont; the Cardinal d'Estouteville hearing arguments about the rehabilitation of Joan; Pierre l'Hermite at study while a messenger kneels in the doorway; the plea of Isabeau d'Arc, Joan of Arc's mother, before a bench of clerics.

The manuscript was thus intended to adapt for a courtly audience the story of Joan of Arc as a noble martyr. It was illuminated by an artist active in Rouen between at least 1525 and 1531, the Ango Hours Master, though it is not in his extravagant 'proto-rococo' vein. The early provenance of the manuscript is not clear: did Diane give the work away, or was it not finally presented to her and kept by someone else? It was owned by Georges d'Amboise (*c.*1500–85), who is not known to have had links with Diane de Poitiers. He was a familiar of Henri II's father, François I, and thus likely to have been in opposition to the Dauphin and his mistress; a cleric, he became Archbishop of Tours in 1547. But he had a daughter, Fleurette d'Armagnac (b.1553), to whom the manuscript was given. She married Blaise de Villemeur in 1565 and used the volume to record details of her family affairs. The lengthy introduction to the text is a panegyric of Diane de Poitiers and refers to her noble past. Perhaps such texts had an educational role in the politics of the French court when Henri II was king, describing to the young an ideal of active womanhood.

See, for the Ango Hours Master, John Plummer, *The Last Flowering: French Painting in Manuscripts, 1420–1530* (Oxford, 1982); on Joan's changing reputation, see Gerd Krumeich, *Jeanne d'Arc in der Geschichte* (Sigmaringen, 1989)

Right: f.10 Trial of Joan of Arc
Below: f.58 Cardinal d'Estouteville listening to the arguments of lawyers.

A Tous vrays fidelles et cheualliers de la foy
catholique. Pierre Reuerend pere en dieu.
Monsieur leuesque de Beauuays. Et reli
gieuse personne. Frere Jehan le maistre.
De lordre des freres prescheurs. Par honorable et discrette
personne. Maistre Jehan grauerent. Venerable docteur
en theologie. Et depute par nostre sainct pere le pape Jn
quisiteur de la foy. Et de toute heresie par tout le Royaul
me de france. Et vicaire commis et ordonne au diocese de
Rouen et specialement a ce present proces. Iceulx delleguez

11

The Survival and Revival of the Illuminator's Craft

We have seen that the medieval art and craft of illumination still had a role in the first decades of the age of the printed book. The expectation that books should be multicoloured did not change overnight; even after printers developed ways of variegating the text with decorative initials of various sizes, printed in black and red, the tradition of colour to guide the eye lived on. For more than a hundred years, for instance, red lines were ruled by hand beneath each line of text in such works as Bibles. Nevertheless, the black-and-white aesthetic became dominant, with both printed books and engravings leaving the press with minimal further intervention by hand. Dürer's prints, for example, are seldom coloured, and the same is true for most printed Books of Hours, which are replete with illustration and ornament. Against this background, groups of illuminators survived by producing books for the luxury end of the market that printers could not emulate – the 1520s Hours workshop, the 'Ghent–Bruges' school and Florentine Books of Hours are examples of these.

For some specialized activities, however, illumination continued to be necessary. There were official documents that needed a prestigious format to give solemnity to the public rituals associated with them. From Cambridge and

113 Patent of nobility for Hernando de Almonte and his brothers, illuminated by Jerónimo Rodriguez. Spain (Granada), 1626.

114 Decollation of St Paul, by Vincenzo Raimondi (Vincent Raymond), in a 19th-century collage of fragments from a choirbook made for the Sistine Chapel under Pope Clement VII. Italy (Rome), *c.*1523–34.

Oxford colleges to the Guilds of the City of London, illuminators were employed to decorate important deeds. Other official documents, from royal letters patent in England to copies of the oaths taken by Venetian doges and councillors, continued to be illuminated up to the eighteenth century.

In Spain, a tradition was maintained of illuminating *cartas de hidalguía*, official confirmations of nobility. In an environment where the nobility were entitled to exemption from certain taxes and were granted legal privileges, the regional royal chanceries of the kingdom could, after officially authenticated research, testify to the status and purity of the suppliant family. These documents also guaranteed that the postulants had no trace of Jewish or Islamic blood, and were thus fitted to uphold the values of monarchical Spain. The ornament in *cartas de hidalguía* tends towards simplified versions of 'Ghent–Bruges' styles, doubtless inherited from manuscripts imported from the Low Countries, with an admixture of Baroque elements (strapwork cartouches, extravagant floral swags and grandiose military insignia of a classical kind, for example) that were becoming standard for those who sought up-to-date fashions.

Some were executed by painters rather than decorative artists. The painter Jerónimo Rodriguez de Espinosa (1562–after 1640), who was active in the region of Valencia after his arrival there from Valladolid in 1596, provided a magnificent work for Hernando de Almonte

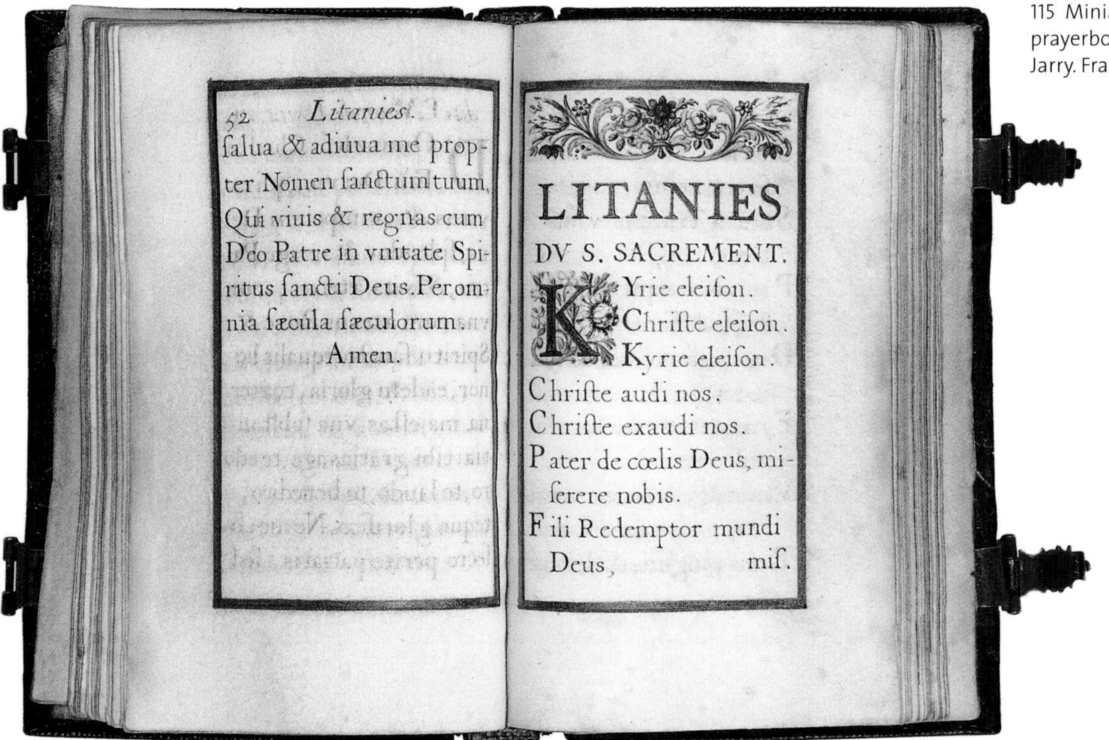
52 Litanies.
ſalua & adiuua me prop-
ter Nomen ſanctum tuum,
Qui viuis & regnas cum
Deo Patre in vnitate Spi-
ritus ſancti Deus. Per omnia ſæcula ſæculorum.
Amen.

LITANIES
DV S. SACREMENT.
Kyrie eleiſon.
Chriſte eleiſon.
Kyrie eleiſon.
Chriſte audi nos.
Chriſte exaudi nos.
Pater de cœlis Deus, mi-
ſerere nobis.
Fili Redemptor mundi
Deus, miſ.

115 Miniature illuminated prayerbook written by Nicolas Jarry. France (Paris), 1661.

of Seville, who with his two brothers gained a charter confirming his nobility, lineage and racial purity in 1626 (a complete family history was included in the text). The document had an impression in lead of the Granada Chancery royal seal of Philip IV (there are details of its registration in Seville and Salteras) and a spectacular red-velvet binding. It opens in the conventional way for such documents (plate 113), with the family arms, the kneeling figures of the beneficiaries (here we see Hernando de Almonte and his wife), the figure of St James driving the Infidel from Spain, all above the suscription: '*Don Phelipe, Por la Gracia de Dios . . .*'. The ornament shows the conventional Baroque ornament of the day, with strapwork cartouches, festoons of flowers, and chubby winged putti.

That calligraphy and illumination continued to be prized is also demonstrated by a number of works produced for the imperial court when it was based in Prague. Georg Hoefnagel (1542–1601) and his son Jakob (1575–*c.*1630) worked as illuminators for Emperor Rudolf II (r.1576–1612), adding illustrations to writing books that had been made for his ancestors Ferdinand I in 1561–62 and Maximilian II in 1571–73 (an interesting reflection on the prestige of such works). To the writing book of 1561–62 were added pictures of plants and animals of breathtaking vividness to satisfy the emperor's interest in the marvels of the natural world and the virtuoso capacity of artists to imitate them (the manuscripts are now in the Getty Museum in Malibu, California, and in the Kunsthistorisches Museum, Vienna).

Churches continued to need liturgical books, particularly choirbooks, that were more economically produced as single copies than in multiples by the printing press. The choirbooks for the Sistine Chapel in the Vatican are just one example of sets of illuminated manuscripts that were regularly added to. For them, the Medici Pope, Leo X (r.1513–21) employed Matteo da Milano among others, while his successors had works illuminated by such artists as the Florentine Jacopo del Giallo and, above all, Vincenzo Raimondi (the Frenchman Vincent Raymond) from the 1530s to the 1550s – in 1549 Paul III called him 'our illuminator [*miniatorem*] for the Chapel and Sacristy, for life' (plate 114). The earliest works of the great French calligrapher and illuminator Nicolas Jarry (*c.*1605–*c.*1666) were commissioned for the church by the Bishop of Meaux and, it seems, by Cardinal Richelieu, the virtual ruler of France. By 1640 it became fashionable for noble ladies to have such works in their private chapels.

These exquisite books were also taken up in the literary

116 Missal given to the Comte de Chambord by the Dames Légitimistes de France. France (Paris), 1844.

sphere. The most famous illuminated manuscript in this milieu was the *Guirlande de Julie* of 1640, which contained poems produced for the Salon of the Marquise de Rambouillet. The V&A manuscript by Jarry, a small prayerbook dated 1661 in a chaste, black binding (plate 115), shows the quality of the writing – the ornament may well be by Jarry, though it is known that other painters were sometimes called on to supply decoration. Jarry's scripts show the interest in improving letter forms that became part of a government initiative after the establishment of the Imprimerie Royale (later the Imprimerie Nationale) in 1640. Ownership of prayerbooks such as these became widespread at the royal court, and illuminated service books were made for the private chapel of the French royal family throughout the eighteenth century. Inmates of the Invalides palace in Paris were put to writing and decorating manuscripts. Books of Hours made for Louis XIV dated 1688 and 1693 were among their products. Since Jarry died at the Invalides, it suggests that he had some role there, perhaps directing the thirty-six scribes who are known to have been active in the institution. Together, they set a standard which prompted growing dissatisfaction with the Garamond type used by the Imprimerie Royale, resulting in the issue of Grandjean's reformed version in 1702.

During the eighteenth century, medieval books began to be admired by one or two collectors on account of their illumination: the Marquis de Paulmy and the Duc de la Vallière with his librarian, the Abbé Rive, were noteworthy pioneers in promoting illuminated manuscripts as worthy of the serious connoisseur. Though they collected manuscripts by Jarry and his successors, they did not actually commission works, as far as is known. Troubadour painters, so-called on account of their enthusiasm for Romantic visions of the Middle Ages, began from the end of the century to study medieval objects, manuscripts included, and reproduced them in paintings. One such, Pierre Révoil, evidently studied

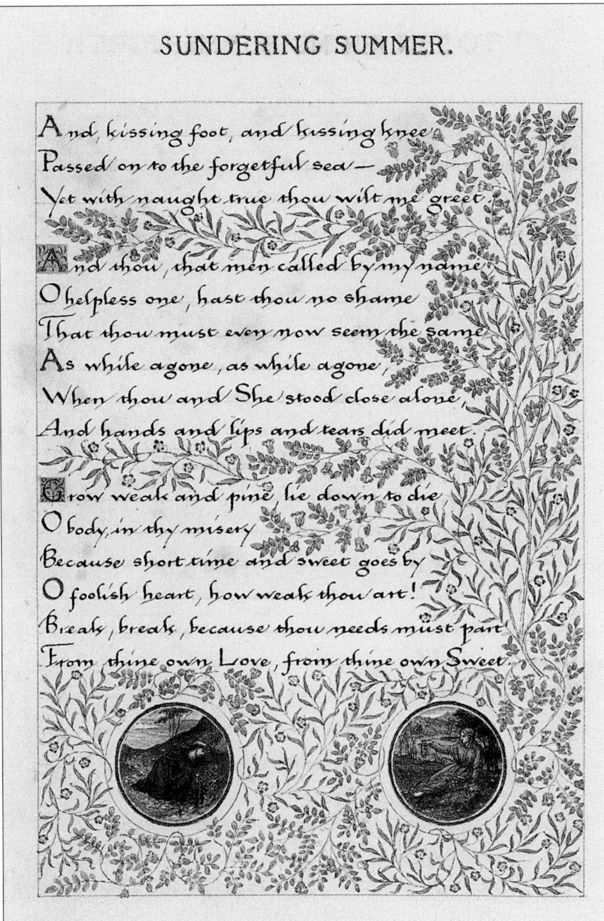

SUNDERING SUMMER.

And, kissing foot, and kissing knee
Passed on to the forgetful sea—
Yet with naught true thou wilt me greet.
And thou, that men called by my name,
O helpless one, hast thou no shame
That thou must even now seem the same
As while agone, as while agone,
When thou and She stood close alone,
And hands and lips and tears did meet.
Grow weak and pine, lie down to die,
O body, in thy misery
Because short time and sweet goes by
O foolish heart, how weak thou art!
Break, break, because thou needs must part
From thine own Love, from thine own Sweet.

117 Book of Verse, by William Morris, Charles Fairfax Murray, Edward Burne-Jones and George Wardle. England (Hammersmith), 1870.

illumination: in 1804 he sent a letter in the form of an illuminated sheet to his colleague Fleury Richard, with extravagant border decoration based on that in fifteenth-century manuscripts, and with mock-medieval language to match. He was also inclined to write to friends in Gothic scripts. This activity was matched by that of the Catholic A.W.N. Pugin in England in the 1830s.

Professional illumination began to develop in Paris in the 1840s as an emulation of medieval practice. Two works in the V&A collection illustrate this development. The first was a Missal made for the Comte de Chambord when he became the head of the House of Bourbon in 1844 on the death of his uncle, Louis Antoine de Bourbon (plate 116). The Missal was financed by the Dames Légitimistes ('Legitimist Ladies of France'), as a token of support for the family that had been driven from power by the Revolution of 1830. The miniatures in the Missal make clear the political programme contained in the gift: Chambord was to emulate those monarchs of the past who had returned from exile to unite France; like Henri IV, he was to unite all parties under the banner of Catholic kingship. The role of the Dames Légitimistes was suggested by references to Joan of Arc: they were to lead the king to fulfil his destiny. This was a well-organized political grouping, and the kind of artefacts they commissioned were replete with political symbolism. When Chambord married in 1846, they commissioned for his wife from Froment-Meurice a dressing table in extravagant Gothic style that was shown to much acclaim at the Great Exhibition of 1851.

This link with conservative Catholicism is also evidenced in a Book of Hours commissioned by Jules Gallois, the self-styled 'Comte de Naives', made between 1838 and 1842. The prefatory section carries a justification for the noble title by citing sixteenth-century documents that mentioned a purported ancestor. It should be remembered that after 1830 the court that had protected noble titles had been abolished, so that those claiming noble status were fearful of imposters – the celebrated instance of this was the Salle des Croisades (Hall of Crusaders) in Versailles, when all who could prove ancestry going back to the crusades could have their arms displayed. Through the efforts of a veritable industry of genealogical research, hosts of claimants appeared. The Hours of the Comte de Naives is replete with his arms, and the illumination by Auguste Ledoux and Charles Leblanc provides a setting that gave them authenticity. While some of the illumination is in popular decorative styles of the nineteenth century, much of it shows careful study of medieval examples, in particular the famous Anne de Bretagne Hours illuminated by Jean Bourdichon before 1508.

The English designer and writer William Morris studied illuminated manuscripts in Oxford and London in the 1850s. By the late 1860s he was producing illuminated versions of the Icelandic sagas that had aroused his enthusiasm. In 1870 he gave Georgiana Burne-Jones a book of poetry written out by himself and containing images and ornament by Edward Burne-Jones, Charles Fairfax Murray and George Wardle (plate 117). Morris was proposing a modern form of illumination in reaction to that used in the conventional art education of the day and to the commercially-led illumination represented by 'do-it-yourself' illuminating manuals and illuminated addresses. These are worth considering, since they form a kind of polarity with the work of collectors and scholars who promoted the introduction of original – medieval –

118 (left) Items from the scrapbook of the designer Miss Gillingham. England, c.1845–65.

119 (above) Illuminated address given by the inhabitants of County Mayo to Captain Whelan. Ireland (Dublin), 1874.

manuscripts to wider audiences through exhibitions. The celebrated Loan Exhibition at South Kensington in 1862, designed to coincide with the London International Exhibition of that year, was the first with a substantial section devote to medieval illuminated manuscripts. It was followed in 1863 by an exhibition devoted solely to these works for the Fellows of the Society of Antiquaries of London.

In the 1840s colour facsimiles of medieval manuscripts had been published by Noel Humphreys and Owen Jones, revelling in the new printing technique of chromolithography. These works were announced as works of a *modern* art – they insisted on their use for purposes of educating designers, and distanced themselves from what many saw as a Roman Catholic art. They were taken up by the new Art Education movement as an important design source. A rather astonishing phenomenon of 1860–61 was the sudden appearance of cheap 'How to illuminate manuals', sold by art publishers and by stationers who produced paints for artists. The succession of editions of the more successful manuals was astonishingly rapid: the manual of John Bradley, published at the end of 1860, was in its eleventh edition by 1863. They were marketed as a worthy domestic leisure pursuit – 'revive the spirit of Giotto and Fra Angelica in your drawing room by illuminating at home' was the tenor of the publicity campaign behind them. It was an art, moreover, that had commercial applications. An album of a jobbing designer, one Miss Gillingham, shows the place that illuminating styles had in her commissions. The album includes some examples of commercially-produced ephemera that copy medieval illumination (plate 118).

Illumination suddenly became the centre of public rituals in the form of the Illuminated Address. These were offered to dignitaries to mark some event, for example retirement, a visit to a borough, the coming-of-age or

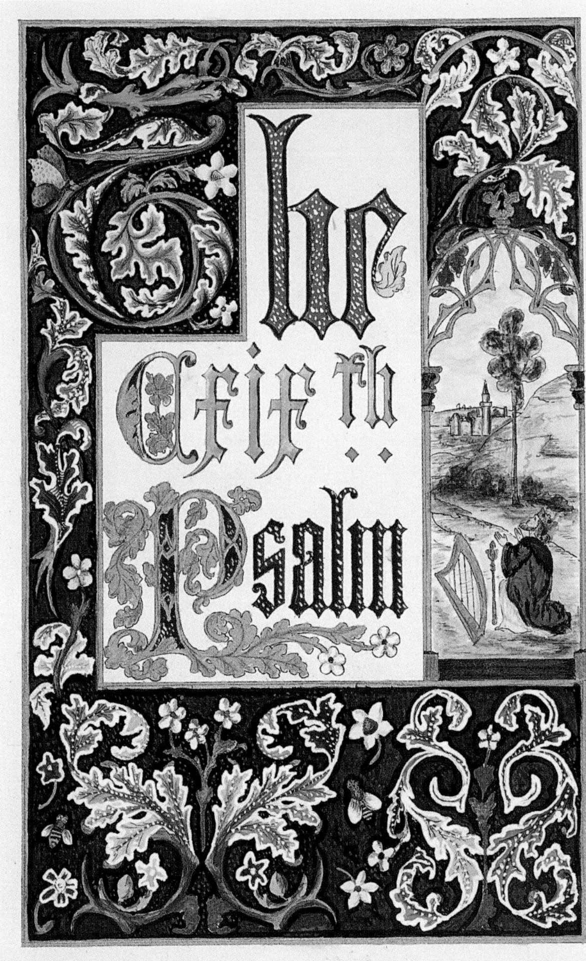

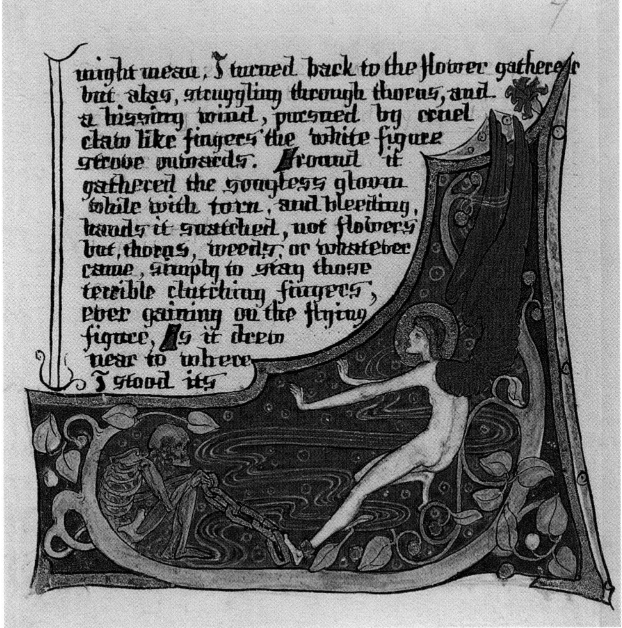

120 (left) Psalm 119, illuminated by David Laurent de Lara and his workforce. England (London), 1866.

121 (above) *The Dream*, illuminated by Phoebe Traquair. Scotland, 1886.

marriage of the estate owner, the gift to a public institution by a benefactor. Such addresses were initially produced by people of some status in the art world, such as Henry Shaw, whose writings on illuminated manuscripts – and his facsimiles of them – had made him an authority. The addresses had sufficient importance to be exhibited publicly: the address presented by the citizens of Dublin to Sir Benjamin Lee Guinness in 1865 was sent to the Exposition Universelle of 1867 in Paris and a reproduction published. Queen Victoria was sent several thousand such addresses for the Jubilees of 1887 and 1897. Characteristic of the genre is the address given to Captain Whelan when he retired as magistrate of County Mayo in Ireland in 1874 (plate 119). Illumination was associated with purity of sentiment, sincerity, loyalty, and was ideal for both public and private gifts and declarations. David Laurent de Lara made a career out of illumination: he published early manuals on how to illuminate, set up the Illuminating Art Union in 1857 with a bevy of noble ladies as patrons, held exhibitions that were reviewed in the *Art Journal*, gave lessons in how to illuminate and employed women to work as illuminators. As regards this last activity, he appears to have been criticized for exploiting his employees: it may be that the illuminated copy of Psalm 119 of 1866, given by one Mary Phillips to a relation, Lewis Phillips, in 1866 was one of their products (plate 120).

This commercial appropriation of illumination meant that it had to be redefined as an art practice. An article in the *Studio* for 1896–97 complained that illuminated addresses were produced by 'ticket-writers and such avowed tradesmen', and that 'vulgarity creeps in at every point'. This sort of response surely lies behind the adoption of illumination as an art form by the Arts and Crafts movement that took its inspiration from William Morris. Illumination was shown at their exhibitions from an early date, produced by people such as Phoebe Traquair (plate 121). Morris and even Ruskin, who had promoted illumination as a purifying art from the 1850s, were both concerned that the integrity, as they saw it, of the medieval illuminator should not be compromised in their own day.

12

Manuscripts in a Museum of Art and Industry: The V&A 'Illuminations' Collection

Printing and books were displayed in the Great Exhibition of 1851. So it was natural that the South Kensington Museum founded in its wake (which in 1899 became the V&A) should collect materials demonstrating how the ornament in books had developed over the centuries. In 1855 J.C. Robinson, the curator who oversaw the growth of the Museum's early collections, declared that the Museum would collect in order to make a survey of every aspect of the ornament of books, from medieval illuminated manuscripts to printed books. The collection was to include 'limited series' of 'characteristic specimens' of every major school of illumination and book design. By 'specimens', it is clear that Robinson intended to collect not complete illuminated books, but single leaves and cuttings that were then freely available on the market, especially in continental Europe.

Robinson's decision marks official sanction of the importance for education of the medieval art form we know as illumination. In the early 1850s medieval manuscripts were tainted with all sorts of unfortunate associations. *Punch* in 1851 had regularly shown cartoons in which illuminated manuscripts were ridiculed as the art of degenerate Catholicism, the enthusiasm of High Church Anglo-Catholics (plate 122). A few art collectors had prized examples of medieval miniatures with their paintings, but these could be accepted as works referred to by the great sixteenth-century historian, Vasari, in his authoritative account of the triumphal progress of painting from Giotto to the art of the High Renaissance. The 1850s was a period of heightened feeling as the Roman Catholic hierarchy was reintroduced into Britain for the first time since the Reformation. The popular

To prevent mistakes, the unilluminated are apprised, that this is simply the letter A.

122 Cartoon from *Punch*, 1851

123 Owen Jones, *Grammar of Ornament* (1856)

press portrayed all aspects of illuminations, so closely associated with Catholic prayerbooks, as a threat to the 'roast-beef Britishness' of native art. It was in fact largely thanks to the work of those prominent in the Art Education movement that illuminated manuscripts joined the ranks of the hallowed examples of early art – such people as Noel Humphreys, Owen Jones and Digby Wyatt in the 1840s pointed to their importance as a source of design and ornament. So it was natural that the museum that enshrined their educational mission should have these works represented.

It is worth stressing the particular mission of the V&A collection of illuminated manuscripts in the nineteenth century. The British Museum library (today the British Library) already had a colossal collection of historical manuscripts and papers, including the library given to the nation by George II as well as the libraries of scholar-aristocrats such as Sir Hans Sloane and Robert Harley; among these were enormous numbers of illuminated manuscripts. The Bodleian library was an academic library with famous medieval holdings; after it had acquired the illuminated manuscripts of the collector and antiquarian Francis Douce, it became as well a point of reference for those interested in art. Private libraries such as those of Samuel Rodgers or Robert Holford, both of them art collectors, similarly had great prestige. These last were dispersed in the saleroom. Private collections such as those of Pierpont Morgan, Henry Walters and Henry Huntingdon in North America ended up as public libraries. In the late nineteenth century, these were some of the richest men in the world and their libraries aimed from the outset to satisfy their notions of art: they commissioned agents in Europe to buy densely illustrated works with a finish that matched their notion of medieval splendour. The collections that libraries put together are very revealing of the assumptions, both conscious and unconscious, of the institutions or individuals who ran them. Those just mentioned serve as a foil to show the originality of what the V&A sought to achieve in the nineteenth century: the American libraries sought to satisfy collectors' notions of artistic excellence, while the V&A aimed to compile an encyclopaedia of art and design in the form of both objects and reproductions, with the specific purpose of raising standards in design in British industry.

What the V&A collected initially were not treasures but fragments of complete manuscripts – originals of a kind that could be circulated in glazed frames to art schools and used by students. The mutilation of medieval books seems to us a barbaric habit, but cut-out leaves were easily available in the art market in the 1850s and before. A famous sale in London in 1825 had included fragments of illuminated manuscripts torn to pieces, so it was said, by Napoleon's troops when they sacked the Sistine Chapel in 1796 (see plate 114). The fragments had been brought to England by an elusive Italian cleric, the Abbate Celotti, and the sale was supported by the most celebrated authority on Italian art of his day, William Ottley, himself a dealer whose private collection included vast numbers of illuminated miniatures cut from medieval books, mostly Italian. When Ottley's collection was dispersed in 1836, its contents were avidly sought by collectors of the day – J.C. Robinson was one of these.

It was as sources of design, however, rather than as art objects or monuments of painting that Robinson collected illumination. He made a series of bulk acquisitions when in Germany in the years 1857 and 1858, buying a series of complete leaves that fulfilled his aim of making a 'representative selection' of medieval styles, even if his preferences directed him chiefly to Italian and German

124 Copy by Henry Shaw from an Anglo-Saxon Gospel Book of *c.*1020 made in Christ Church Canterbury. England (London), *c.*1866–68.

examples (his earlier reference in 1843 to the 'inane compositions and puerile drawings' of Gothic artists indicates a prejudice against works that were not progressing to the perfection of the Renaissance). Robinson in fact was fleshing out the programme elaborated by his colleague Owen Jones, in whose *Grammar of Ornament* of 1856 details from a range of manuscripts between the seventh and seventeenth centuries had been published in colour for students of design (plate 123).

Robinson resigned from the Museum in 1863, though he was retained as an 'art referee' to advise on acquisitions until 1867. As a result Henry Shaw was approached in 1864 to evaluate the 'Illuminations' collection. Shaw's knowledge of medieval art was based on minute study of original artefacts: he had published works on manuscripts, furniture and costume with plates that reproduced details of original objects. Between 1830 and 1833 he had co-operated with Frederick Madden to produce *Illuminated Ornament Selected from Manuscripts*. This work was aimed at the antiquarian and art education market, and significantly presented illumination in terms of ornamental detail. He criticized the V&A collection for its over-representation of German and Italian illumination of the later medieval period: rather than collect expensive originals, he suggested, the Museum should commission him to make copies from a list of famous manuscripts that he could supply. This advice was taken. Shaw already had a business providing facsimiles of manuscripts in the British Museum library, and in the 1860s demand for this kind of work was at its height. The Museum spent nearly £100 in 1866 acquiring facsimile copies of well-known manuscripts, approaching him after a sale in 1866 to order second copies of what had been sold. The facsimiles are truly remarkable in their accuracy as regards composition and colouring. They added a new dimension to the V&A collection by providing examples of Anglo-Saxon illumination (plate 124), of the marvellously inventive English Psalters of the fourteenth century with their anecdotal border ornament (plate 125), and of the famous Bedford Missal, an icon of British history with its portrait of the duke himself (plate 126).

Shaw was not the only person from whom such facsimiles were bought. Lord Thynne, the son of the Marquis of Bath and a canon of Canterbury Cathedral, appears to have turned to illuminating after resigning his offices and defecting to the Roman Catholic church in 1864. Illumination was for him part of a campaign to revive a hallowed medieval art practice. Work by Caleb Wing was also acquired, like Shaw a specialist in the production of facsimiles and earning a living in the printing trade. His facsimile from the Della Rovere Missal, illuminated in Italy in the 1490s by Francesco Bettini (plate 127) was probably made when he repaired the original, damaged by a flood, when it was owned by John Jarman.

The facsimilies were acquired as sources for design, but it is difficult not to see them as art objects too, embodying the moral qualities that Victorians demanded from art. The Museum took pains to have at its disposal facsimilies of miniatures from the choirbooks of Siena Cathedral, borrowed in this case from the National Gallery. These were then attributed to Fra Angelico, a painter whose otherworldy spirituality was promoted by Ruskin as the acme of Italian art (plate 128). In all, the works

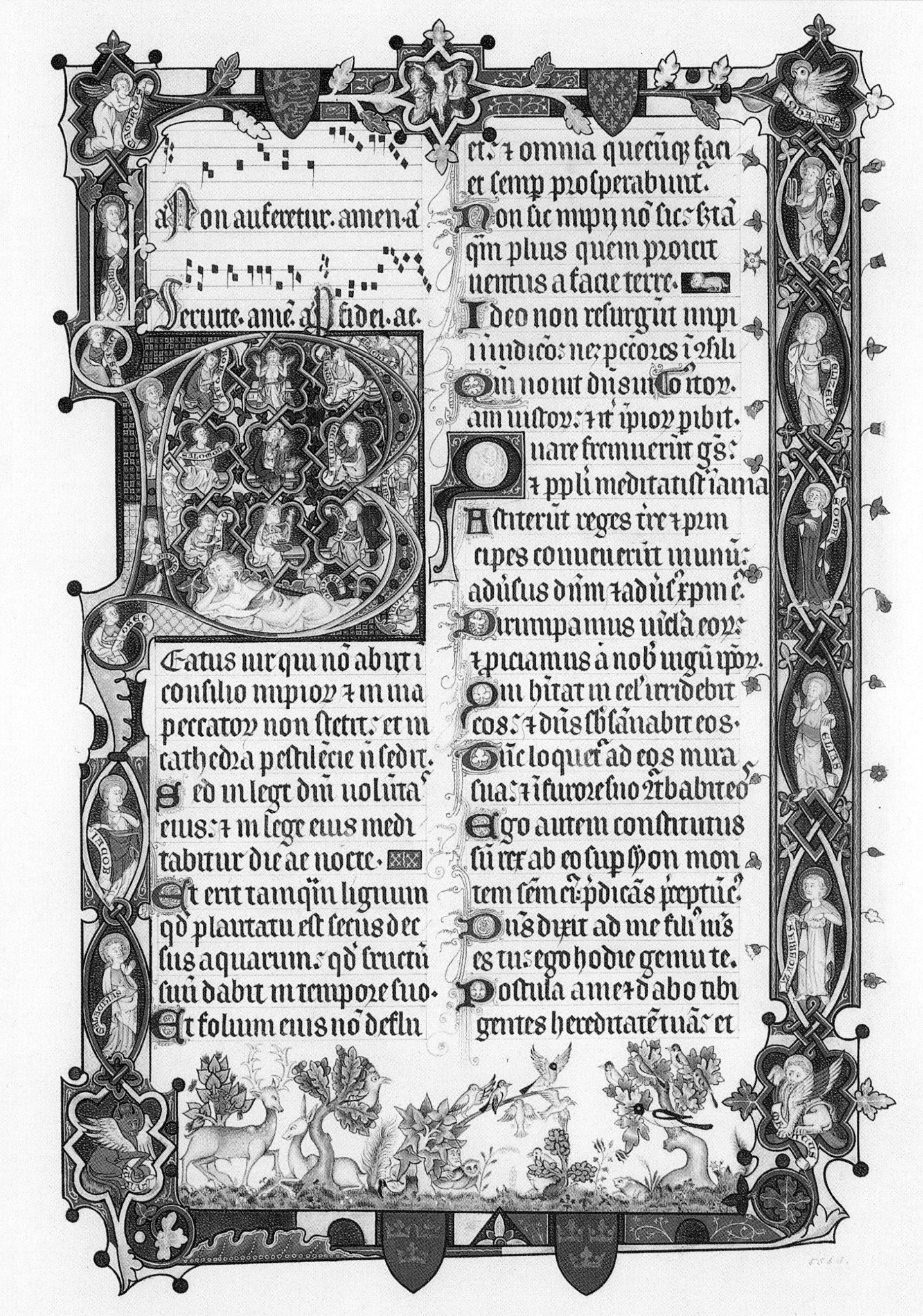

125 (left) Copy by Henry Shaw from the Howard Psalter, made in England in the early 14th century. England (London), *c.*1866–68.

126 (right) Copy by Henry Shaw from the Book of Hours made for the Duke of Bedford ('The Bedford Missal'), made in Paris *c.*1423–30. England (London), *c.*1866–68.

represented in these facsimiles, which came from both private and public collections, were given an iconic status as embodying the purest expression of the illuminator's art, one that operated in a world of spiritual values unsullied by the materialist commercialism of secular affairs.

These facsimiles should be seen as an integral part of the V&A's collection of illumination. In a way, they set the standard that the originals had to reach. Shaw himself stated that, for purposes of study, they were better than originals. At the same time, however, leaves and cuttings from original manuscripts were being bought, often in ready-made collections. The Museum was profiting from the trade in such things that flourished in all European countries – Ruskin's celebrated remark that he spent an evening in 1853 cutting miniatures from manuscripts ('hard work') shows him following this practice. It was recognized that the British Museum library was the national collection of illuminated manuscripts; works acquired for South Kensington were sources of design for students in the art schools around the country.

vous entier
vous entier
vous entier
vous entier
a vous entier
a vous entier
a vous entier
a vous entier
a vous entier

which contemporary typographers were so interested. 'Art works' were more attractive: the cut-out initial signed by the Italian miniaturist Girolamo da Cremona was bought in 1894 for £100, and the leaf from the Eadwine Psalter for the same sum.

The nature of the collection changed in 1902, when the collector William Reid of Dunfermline, a linen manufacturer, lent his collection of eighty-three items to the museum for display and decided to convert the loan into a gift. The gift was particularly suitable in that the bulk of the works were fifteenth-century Books of Hours that were rich in the kind of ornament favoured by the Victorian public. Some outstanding manuscripts came with the bequest of Sir George Salting in 1910, including the Simon Marmion Hours (see pp. 106–7), the Alfonso of Aragon Hours (pp. 100–1), cuttings from the sixteenth-century Sistine Chapel choirbooks that had been owned by Ottley (plate 114), and the prayerbook of Margaret de Foix (pp. 102–3). Illuminated manuscripts came into the Museum through various bequests thereafter. Particularly notable were the acquisitions of James Wardrop in the 1950s, which included a series of fifteenth-century Italian manuscripts in humanistic script by some of the best scribes of that period.

Wardrop's achievement was to add a new dimension to the collection, that of humanistic manuscripts from Renaissance Italy, wilfully avoided by his predecessors. It seems fitting that this scholar, whose interest in book design and typography is shown by his work at the Gregynog Press, should have rounded off the Museum's collection by adding to it just those works that had such an impact on the best typography of the early twentieth century. Wardrop's acquisitions made the V&A's holdings yet more relevant to students and people working in industry who had been the 'target audience' since the 1850s. Additions to the collection after this date have sought to document the working practices of medieval book-makers (see, for instance, the Harreteau Hours; pp. 64–65), to extend the range of scripts represented, and to examine the fate of illuminated manuscripts and illumination in the nineteenth century. Edward Johnston started his celebrated class in calligraphy and lettering at the Royal College of Art in 1899, and his followers established the Society of Scribes and Illuminators, which still flourishes today. Johnston's work is continually on

A few complete manuscripts were acquired, however: in 1865 a choirbook of *c.*1380 from Florence; in 1866 a choirbook dated 1492 from Verona. They were described in terms of the numbers of initials they contained. Apart from these, most complete illuminated manuscripts were acquired on account of their bindings – this had been one of the categories in the 1851 Great Exhibition, and works were acquired to give a historical account of the craft.

The 1890s – the decade of the Aesthetic Movement and the promotion of Beauty for Beauty's sake by such figures as Walter Pater and Oscar Wilde – saw a radical shift in the Museum's view of its role, one in which the collection of objects as documentation (i.e. copies of famous works and examples of industrial art) was tempered by a pressing need to acquire works that were self-standing works of art. The Museum moved away from artisans and manufacturers towards collectors and connoisseurs. The change is particularly evident in the illuminated manuscripts collected during the period when James Weale was Chief Librarian (1890–97): in 1891 the St Denis Missal; in 1896 a large Pliny in humanistic script of the 1460s. It seems odd today that humanistic manuscripts were acquired in such small quantities and with an apparent casualness – the Pliny and manuscripts of Horace and Palladius bought in 1894 were, apart from some Florentine Books of Hours, all the Museum had to demonstrate the principles of book and letter design in

127 (opposite) Copy by Caleb Wing of a historiated initial (Presentation of Christ in the Temple), signed by Francesco Bettini, in the Della Rovere Missal, made in Rome in the 1490s. England, second half of the 19th century.

128 (right) Copy made for the Arundel Society of a historiated initial *R* (Annunciation) by Zanobi Strozzi in a choirbook from St Mark's, Florence. Italy, *c.*1861–62.

view in London: apart from being paraded around the capital on buses and tube trains (he designed the lettering used by London Transport), it can be seen in the V&A's major collection of his work and that by his pupils.

In short, the V&A's collection of illuminated manuscripts was made as part of a great educational enterprise undertaken by the government under the aegis of Henry Cole in the second half of the nineteenth century. It was a collection that was originally aimed at a new kind of audience. It was governed by a distinctly Victorian view of what constituted excellence in design. Roger Fry's criticism of the 1908 Burlington Exhibition of Illuminated Manuscripts, made up, he thought, of gaudy, over-ornate works of the later Middle Ages, signalled an end to the prestige of Victorian historicism. Henceforth, early Romanesque manuscripts could be admired above the Gothic, their simplicity appreciated in an environment conditioned by the austere aesthetic of the Bauhaus in a Europe traumatized by the Great War of 1914–18. Today, we do not apply such confident value judgements, and are acutely aware of what both early and late illumination have to tell us about the visual culture of the Middle Ages, the factors that governed its production, and the history of different ways in which it has been appreciated.

ILLUSTRATION SOURCES

The illuminated manuscripts reproduced in this book were acquired by the Museum as part of a single collecting campaign that began in the 1850s. Since 1908, when the department known until very recently as the Prints, Drawings and Paintings Collection was split off from the library, all works in volume format have been kept in the National Art Library (NAL), while single leaves and fragments ('cuttings') went to the new department (PDP). Both NAL and PDP are now part of the V&A's Word and Image Department, established in 2002.

Plates

1 NAL, MSL/1983/18/3 (detail)
2 NAL, MSL/1980/72, f.26 (detail)
3 NAL, MSL/1902/1683 (Reid 41), f.91v (detail)
4 PDP E.378-1911 (detail)
5 NAL, MSL/1984/44 (detail)
6 NAL, MSL/1918/475, f.202 (detail)
7 NAL, MSL/1921/1721, f.8 (detail)
8 NAL, MSL/1950/2464, f.46v (detail)
9 NAL, MSL/1954/1609, ff.120v-121 (detail)
10 NAL, MSL/1946/1485, f.16v
11 Berlin, Staatsbibliothek, Ms. lat. 2° 384. See *The Library*, Fourth Series, vol. IX, no.4 (March 1929), p.380 and plate
12 PDP, 8985 B (detail)
13 PDP, 8984 B
14 PDP, 8984 A
15 PDP, 8985 C
16 PDP, 244.2 (detail)
17 NAL, MSL/1870/7789, f.96 (detail)
18. NAL, MSL/1980/174, f.57v (detail)
19. PDP, E.397-1892 (detail)
20. PDP, 8987 C
21. PDP E.372-1911
22. NAL, MSL/1902/1696 (Reid 55), f. 140 (detail)
23. NAL, MSL/1984/29, f.112 (detail)
24. NAL, MSL/1980/174, f.60v (detail)
25. NAL, MSL/1902/1663 (Reid 23), f. 1 (detail)
26. NAL, MSL/1891/1346, f. 191 (detail)
27. NAL, MSL/1918/475, f.67 (detail)
28. NAL, MSL/1902/1670 (Reid 34), f.13 (detail)
29. Göttingen, Niedersächsiche Staats- und Landesbibliothek, Cod. Uffenbach 51, ff.10v-11. See Hellmut Lehmann-Haupt, ed., *The Göttingen model book. A facsimile edition* (Columbia: University of Missouri Press, 1972)
30. PDP, 279.6
31. NAL, MSL/1950/2464, f.47 (detail)
32. NAL, MSL/1956/366, f.1 (detail)
33. NAL, MSL/1894/534, f.2 (detail)
34. NAL, MSL/1947/101, f.162 (detail)
35. NAL, MSL/1866/4929, f.81 (detail)
36. NAL, MSL/1902/1697 (Reid 56), f.36v (detail).
37. NAL, MSL/1902/1696 (Reid 55), f. 217v (detail)
38. NAL, MSL/1902/1699 (Reid 66), f.217v (detail)
39. NAL, MSL/1891/1346, f.96v (detail)
40. NAL, MSL/1866/25.1, f.1
41. NAL, MSL 1902/2074 (Reid 83), f.54 (detail)
42. NAL, MSL/1891/1346, f.370 (detail).
43. NAL, MSL/1891/1346, f.295v (detail)
44. PDP, 1547
45. NAL, MSL/1902/1646 (Reid 4), f.56v (detail)
46. NAL, MSL/1894/181, f.48 (detail)
47. NAL, MSL/1902/1646 (Reid 4), f.16 (detail)
48. PDP, 433
49. D.1146-1881
50. PDP, 4918.7
51. PDP, 8122
52. NAL, MSL/1891/1346, f.440 (detail)
53. NAL, MSL/1918/475, f.192v (detail)
54. NAL, MSL/1902/1662 (Reid 20), f. 35
55. NAL, MSL/1902/1683 (Reid 41), f.9 (detail)
56. PDP, 1107.19
57. NAL, MSL/1902/1670 (Reid 34), f.29v (detail)
58. NAL, MSL/1902/1707 (Reid 64), f.33
59. NAL, MSL/1954/1609, f.1
60. PDP, 4918.1
61. NAL, MSL/1910/2386 (Salting 1223), ff.18v-19
62. NAL, MSL/1947/101, f.10 (detail)
63. PDP, E.4579-1910
64. NAL, MSL/1981/39, f.63
65. PDP, 254.1
66. PDP, 8997 C
67. PDP, 8992
68. NAL, MSL/1902/2074 (Reid 83), f.45 (detail)
69. NAL, MSL/1891/1346 ff.28, 64, 92, 67v.
70. NAL, NAL, MSL/1902/1654 (Reid 11), ff.39, 29, 87v (details)
71. NAL, MSL/1902/2074 (Reid 83), ff.31v (detail)
72. NAL, MSL/1902/2074 (Reid 83), ff.19v-20
73. NAL, MSL/1891/1346, f.236
74. NAL, MSL/1891/1346, f. 259v
75. NAL, MSL/1894/181, f.67v
76. NAL, MSL/1902/1684 (Reid 42), f.46
77. NAL, MSL/1902/1662 (Reid 20), f.47
78. NAL, MSL/1902/1698 (Reid 65), f.27
79. NAL, MSL 1902/1696 (Reid 55), f. 89
80. PDP, D.332-1893
81. PDP, 9027
82. PDP, D.334-1893
83. PDP, 4925
84. PDP, 817-1894
85. PDP, 799-1894
86. PDP, E.1186-1921
87. PDP, 4140, 4142
88. PDP, E.159-1910
89. PDP, E.366-1892 to E.371-1892 (three bifolia), with other gatherings from the same MS lying flat (E.3611892 to E.4121892)
90. NAL, MSL/1902/1698 (Reid 65), ff.51v-52
91. NAL, MSL/1902/1698 (Reid 65), ff. 53v, 71, 26
92. NAL, MSL/1993/2, f.16v.
93. NAL, MSL/1993/2, f.18v
94. NAL, MSL/1993/2, f.67v.
95. NAL, MSL/1993/2, f.80v.
96. NAL, MSL/1993/2, f.50v
97. NAL, MSL/1984/29, f.48
98. NAL, MSL/1918/475, f.67
99. NAL, MSL/1902/1654 (Reid 11), f.50v
100. PDP, E.687-1918
101. NAL, MSL/1918/475, f.59v
102. PDP, E.710-1918
103. NAL, MSL/1918/475, f.64
104. PDP, 279.6
105. Paris, Bibliothèque nationale de France, Kh.25 rés. See Max Geisberg, *Das älteste gestochene deutsche Kartenspiel vom Meister der Spielkarten* (Strassburg, 1905), p.37, no.15, Plate 8
106. NAL, MSL/1902/1677 (Reid 22), ff.5v-6
107. NAL, MSL/1902/1690 (Reid 45), f.36v
108. NAL, MSL/1902/1690 (Reid 45), f.41v (detail)
109. NAL, MSL/1902/1667 (Reid 32), ff.83v-84
110. Nuremberg, Germanisches Nationalmuseum, L.5. See Renger, Marta, 'The Netherlandish Grisaille miniatures: some unexplored aspects', *Wallraf-Richartz-Jahrbuch*, Band XLIV (1983), p.163
111. NAL, pressmark RC.F.20, sig. a2 (ISTC no. ip01052200)
112. NAL, pressmark BD 41
113. NAL, MSL/1981/11, ff.vi verso-1
114. PDP, E.4578-1910.
115. NAL, MSL/1949/1171, pp.52-3
116. NAL, MSL/1984/68. ff.18v-19
117. NAL, MSL/1953/131
118. NAL, MSL/1988/13
119. NAL, 1983/21
120. NAL, MSL/1961/2030, f.2
121. NAL, MSL/1936/1765, f.7
122. NAL, *Punch,* vol. XXI (1851), p.164
123. NAL, pressmark 111.Q.18
124. PDP, 5869
125. PDP, 5863
126. PDP, 5892
127. PDP, D.310-1899
128. PDP, E.120-1996

References for Chapter 10, 'A Procession of Manuscripts'

1. PDP, 816-1894
2. PDP, 9037 D
3. NAL, MSL/1983/19
4. PDP, 8986 C, E
5. NAL, MSL/1902/2074 (Reid 83)
6. PDP., 9036 E, W
7. PDP, 8997.I
8. NAL, MSL/1891/1346
9. PDP, 432, 3045
10. NAL, MSL/1902/1646 (Reid 4)
11. PDP, E.4582-1910; E.4583-1910
12. NAL, MSL/1947/101
13. NAL, MSL/1910/2387 (Salting 1224)
14. NAL, MSL/1910/2385 (Salting 1222)
15. PDP, 1107.1, 1107.3
16. NAL, MSL/1910/2384 (Salting 1221)
17. MSL 1949/1253
18. PDP, 274.2
19. NAL, MSL/1954/1609 (Cicero), L.1934/1791 (Caesar)
20. NAL, MSL/1910/2388 (Salting 1861). Printed Book of Hours: NAL pressmark RC.H.13
21. NAL, MSL/1922/1722
22. NAL, MSL/1921/1721
23. NAL, MSL/1999/6. Acquired with the generous support of the Friends of the National Libraries
24. NAL, MSL/1981/39
25. NAL, MSL/1998/3

List of National Art Library manuscripts by MS inventory number

MSL/1866/25.1, f.1. Plate 40
MSL/1866/4929, f.81 (detail). Plate 35
MSL/1870/7789, f.96 (detail). Plate 17
MSL/1891/1346. Pages 90-91
ff.28, 64, 92, 67v. Plate 69
f.96v (detail). Plate 39
f.191 (detail). Plate 26
f.236. Plate 73
f.259v. Plate 74
f.295v (detail). Plate 43
f.370 (detail). Plate 42
f.440 (detail). Plate 52
MSL/1894/181, f.48 (detail). Plate 46
MSL/1894/181, f.67v. Plate 75
MSL/1894/534, f.2 (detail). Plate 33
MSL/1902/1646 (Reid 4). Pages 94-5
f.16 (detail). Plate 47
f.56v (detail). Plate 45
MSL/1902/1654 (Reid 11), ff.39, 29, 87v (details). Plate 70
f.50v. Plate 99
MSL/1902/1662 (Reid 20), f. 35. Plate 54
f.47. Plate 77
MSL/1902/1663 (Reid 23), f.1 (detail). Plate 25
MSL/1902/1667 (Reid 32), ff.83v-84. Plate 109
MSL/1902/1670 (Reid 34), f.13 (detail). Plate 28
f.29v (detail). Plate 57
MSL/1902/1677 (Reid 22), ff.5v-6. Plate 106
MSL/1902/1683 (Reid 41), f.9 (detail). Plate 55
f.91v (detail). Plate 3
MSL/1902/1684 (Reid 42), f.46. Plate 76
MSL/1902/1690 (Reid 45), f.36v. Plate 107
f.41v (detail). Plate 108
MSL 1902/1696 (Reid 55), f.89. Plate 79
f.140 (detail). Plate 22
f.217v (detail). Plate 37
MSL/1902/1697 (Reid 56), f.36v (detail). Plate 36
MSL/1902/1698 (Reid 65), f.27. Plate 78
ff.51v-52. Plate 90
ff. 53v, 71, 26. Plate 91
MSL/1902/1699 (Reid 66), f.217v (detail). Plate 38
MSL/1902/1707 (Reid 64), f.33. Plate 58
MSL/1902/2074 (Reid 83). Pages 84-85
ff.19v-20. Plate 72
f.31v (detail). Plate 71
f.45 (detail). Plate 68
f.54 (detail). Plate 41
MSL/1910/2384 (Salting 1221). Pages 106-7
MSL/1910/2385 (Salting 1222). Pages 102-3
MSL/1910/2386, ff.18v-19. Plate 61
MSL/1910/2387 (Salting 1224). Pages 100-1
MSL/1910/2388 (Salting 1861). Pages 114-15
MSL/1918/475, f.59v. Plate 101
f.64. Plate 103
f.67 (detail). Plate 27
f.67. Plate 98
f.192v (detail). Plate 53
f.202 (detail). Plate 6
MSL/1921/1721. Pages 118-19
f.8 (detail). Plate 7
MSL/1922/1722. Pages 116-17
MSL/1936/1765, f.7. Plate 121
MSL/1946/1485, f.16v. Plate 10
MSL/1947/101. Pages 98-9
f.10 (detail). Plate 62
f.162 (detail). Plate 34
MSL/1949/1171 pp.52-3. Plate 115
MSL 1949/1253. Pages 108-9
MSL/1950/2464, f.46v (detail). Plate 8
f.47 (detail). Plate 31
MSL/1953/131. Plate 117
MSL/1954/1609. Pages 112-13
f.1. Plate 59
ff.120v-121. Plate 9
MSL/1956/366, f.1 (detail). Plate 32
MSL/1961/2030, f.2. Plate 120
MSL/1980/72, f.26 (detail). Plate 2
MSL/1980/174, f.57v (detail). Plate 18
f.60v (detail). Plate 24
MSL/1981/11, ff.vi verso-1. Plate 113
MSL/1981/39. Pages 122-3
f.63. Plate 64
MSL/1983/19. Pages 80-81
MSL/1983/21. Plate 119
MSL/1983/18/3 (detail). Plate 1
MSL/1984/29, f.48. Plate 97
f.112 (detail). Plate 23
MSL/1984/44 (detail). Plate 5
MSL/1984/68. ff.18v-19. Plate 116
MSL/1988/13. Plate 118
MSL/1993/2, f.16v. Plate 92
f.18v. Plate 93
f.50v. Plate 96
f.67v. Plate 94
f.80v. Plate 95
MSL/1998/3. Pages 124-5
MSL/1999/6. Pages 120-21

NAL Printed Books

Pressmark 111.Q.18. Plate 123
Pressmark RC.F.20, sig. a2 (ISTC no. ip01052200). Plate 111
Pressmark RC.H.13. Pages 114-15
Pressmark BD 41. Plate 112
L.1934/1791 (Caesar). Pages 112-13
Punch, vol. XXI (1851), p.164. Plate 122

List of National Art Library MSS by Collection Number

Reid 4 (MSL/1902/1646) Pages 94-5
f.16 (detail). Plate 47
f.56v (detail). Plate 45
Reid 11 (MSL/1902/1654), ff.39, 29, 87v (details). Plate 70
f.50v. Plate 99
Reid 20 (MSL/1902/1662), f. 35. Plate 54
f.47. Plate 77
Reid 22 (MSL/1902/1677), ff.5v-6. Plate 106
Reid 23 (MSL/1902/1663), f.1 (detail). Plate 25
Reid 32 (MSL/1902/1667), ff.83v-84. Plate 109
Reid 34 (MSL/1902/1670), f.13 (detail). Plate 28
f.29v (detail). Plate 57
Reid 41 (MSL/1902/1683), f.9 (detail). Plate 55
f.91v (detail). Plate 3
Reid 42 (MSL/1902/1684), f.46. Plate 76
Reid 45 (MSL/1902/1690), f.36v. Plate 107
f.41v (detail). Plate 108
Reid 55 (MSL 1902/1696), f. 89. Plate 79
f. 140 (detail). Plate 22
f. 217v (detail). Plate 37
Reid 56 (MSL/1902/1697), f.36v (detail). Plate 36
Reid 65 (MSL/1902/1698), f.27. Plate 78
ff.51v-52. Plate 90
ff. 53v, 71, 26. Plate 91
Reid 66 (MSL/1902/1699), f.217v (detail). Plate 38
Reid 64 (MSL/1902/1707), f.33 (detail). Plate 58
Reid 83 (MSL/1902/2074). Pages 84-5
ff.19v-20. Plate 72
f.31v (detail). Plate 71
f.45 (detail). Plate 68
f.54 (detail). Plate 41
Salting 1221 (MSL/1910/2384). Pages 106-7
Salting 1222 (MSL/1910/2385). Pages 102-3
Salting 1223 (MSL/1910/2386), ff.18v-19. Plate 61
Salting 1224 (MSL/1910/2387). Pages 100-1
Salting 1861 (MSL/1910/2388). Pages 114-15

Prints, Drawings and Paintings Collection Inventory Numbers

274.2. Pages 110-11
244.2 (detail). Plate 16
254.1. Plate 65
279.6. Plate 104
279.6. Plate 30
432. Pages 92-3
433. Plate 48
1107.1. Pages 104-5
1107.3. Pages 104-5
1107.19. Plate 56
1547. Plate 44
3045. Pages 92-3
4140, 4142. Plate 87
4918.1. Plate 60
4918.7. Plate 50
4925. Plate 83
5863. Plate 125
5869. Plate 124
5892. Plate 126
8122. Plate 51
8984 A. Plate 14
8984 B. Plate 13
8985 B (detail). Plate 12
8985 C. Plate 15
8986 C, E. Pages 82-3
8987 C. Plate 20
8992. Plate 67
8997 C. Plate 66
8997.I. Pages 88-9
9027. Plate 81
9036 E, W. Pages 86-7
9037 D. Pages 78-9
D.1146-1881. Plate 49
E.366-1892 to E.371-1892 (three bifolia), with other gatherings from the same MS lying flat (E.361-1892 to E.412-1892). Plate 89
E.397-1892 (detail). Plate 19
D.332-1893. Plate 80
D.334-1893. Plate 82
799-1894. Plate 85
816-1894. Pages 76-7
817-1894. Plate 84
D.310-1899. Plate 127
E.159-1910. Plate 88
E.4578-1910. Plate 114
E.4579-1910. Plate 63
E.4582-1910, Pages 96-7
E.4583-1910. Pages 96-7
E.372-1911. Plate 21
E.378-1911(detail). Plate 4
E.687-1918. Plate 100
E.710-1918. Plate 102
E.1186-1921. Plate 86
E.120-1996. Plate 128

Manuscripts and prints from other libraries:

Berlin, Staatsbibliothek, Ms. lat. 2° 384. See *The Library*, Fourth Series, vol. IX, no.4 (March 1929), p.380 and plate. Plate 11

Göttingen, Niedersächsiche Staats- und Landesbibliothek, Cod. Uffenbach 51, ff.10v-11. See Hellmut Lehmann-Haupt, ed., *The Göttingen model book. A facsimile edition* (Columbia: University of Missouri Press, 1972). Plate 29

Nuremberg, Germanisches Nationalmuseum, L.5. See Renger, Marta, 'The Netherlandish Grisaille miniatures: some unexplored aspects', *Wallraf-Richartz-Jahrbuch*, Band XLIV (1983), p.163. Plate 110

Paris, Bibliothèque nationale de France, Kh.25 rés. See Max Geisberg, *Das älteste gestochene deutsche Kartenspiel vom Meister der Spielkarten* (Strassburg, 1905), p.37, no.15, Plate 8. Plate 105

SELECT BIBLIOGRAPHY

Alexander, J.J.G., *Medieval Illuminators and Their Methods of Work* (Yale University Press, 1992)

— ed., *The Painted Page: Italian Renaissance Book Illumination, 1450–1550* (Munich and New York, 1994)

L'Art au temps des rois maudits: Philippe le Bel et ses fils, 1285–1328 (Paris, 1998)

Avril, François, *Manuscript Painting at the Court of France, 1310–1380* (London, 1978)

Backhouse, Janet, *The Illuminated Page: Ten Centuries of Manuscript Painting in the British Library* (London, 1997)

Bischoff, Bernhard, *Latin Palaeography: Antiquity and the Middle Ages* (Cambridge, 1990)

Brown, Michelle, *A Guide to Western Historical Scripts from Antiquity to 1600* (London, 1990)

Calkins, 'Stages of execution: procedures of illumination as revealed in an unfinished Book of Hours', *Gesta*, vol. XVII, no.1 (1978), pp. 61–70

Camille, Michael, *Image on the Edge: The Margins of Medieval Art* (London, 1992)

De Hamel, Christopher, *Glossed Books of the Bible and the Origin of the Paris Booktrade* (Woodbridge, 1984)

— *A History of Illuminated Manuscripts* (Oxford, 1986; 2nd ed. London, 1993)

—*The Book: A History of the Bible* (London, 2002)

Delaissé, L.M.J., 'The importance of Books of Hours for the history of the medieval book', *Gatherings in Honor of Dorothy E. Miner* (Baltimore, 1974)

Farquhar, James Douglas, 'Identity in an anonymous age: Bruges manuscript illuminators and their signs', *Viator*, vol. XI (1980), pp. 371–83, figs 1–12

Griffiths, Jeremy, *Book Production and Publishing in Britain, 1374–1475* (Cambridge, 1989)

Gumbert, J.P., *The Dutch and their Books in the Manuscript Age* (London, 1990)

Hellinga, Lotte, and J.B. Trapp, eds, *The Book in Britain, 1400–1557*, vol. III of *The Cambridge History of the Book* (Cambridge, 1999)

Hindman, Sandra, ed., *Printing the Written Word: The Social History of Books, 1450–1520* (Ithaca, NY, and London, 1991)

Hindman, Sandra, Michael Camille, Nina Rowe and Rowan Watson, *Manuscript Illumination in the Modern Age* (Evanston, IL, 2001)

Light, Laura, 'French Bibles, *c.*1200–1230: a new look at the origin of the Paris Bible', *The Early Medieval Bible: Its Production, Decoration and Use*, ed. R. Gameson (Cambridge, 1994)

Marrow, James, *et al.*, eds, *Golden Age of Dutch Manuscript Painting* (Stuttgart, 1989)

Meiss, Millard, *French Painting in the Time of Jean de Berry: The Boucicaut Master* (London, 1968)

— *French Painting in the Time of Jean de Berry: The Late Fourteenth Century and the Patronage of the Duke*, 2nd ed. (London, 1969)

— *French Painting in the Time of Jean de Berry: The Limbourgs and Their Contemporaries*, 2 vols (London, 1974)

Munby, A.N.L., *Connoisseurs and Medieval Miniatures, 1750–1850* (Oxford, 1972)

Randall, Lilian M.C., *Images in the Margins of Gothic Manuscripts* (Berkeley, 1966)

Renger, Marta, 'The Netherlandish grisaille miniatures: some unexplored aspects', *Wallraf-Richartz-Jahrbuch*, vol. XLIV (1984), pp. 145–73

Reynaud, N. and F. Avril, *Les Manuscrits à peintures en France, 1440–1520* (Paris, 1993)

Rouse, Richard H., and Mary A. Rouse, *Manuscripts and their Makers: Commercial Book Producers in Medieval Paris, 1200–1500* (Turnhout, 2000)

Sandler, Lucy Freeman, *Gothic Manuscripts, 1285–1385*, 2 vols (London, 1986), part V of *Survey of Manuscripts Illuminated in the British Isles*, ed. J.J.G. Alexander

Scott, Kathleen, *Later Gothic Manuscripts, 1390–1490*, 2 vols (London, 1997), part VI of *Survey of Manuscripts Illuminated in the British Isles*, ed. J.J.G. Alexander (London, 1996)

Sterling, Charles, *La Peinture médiévale à Paris, 1300–1500*, 2 vols (Paris, 1987–90)

Watson, Rowan, *Illumination and Illuminated Manuscripts in the 19th Century: A Survey of Responses in England, France and Germany to the Revival of a Medieval Art Form* (London, National Library], 1997) [reproduced typescript]

— 'Educators, collectors, fragments and the "Illuminations" collection at the Victoria and Albert Museum in the nineteenth century', *Interpreting and Collecting Fragments of Medieval Books*, ed. Linda Brownrigg and Margaret M. Smith (Los Altos Hills, CA, and London, 2000)

Wieck, Roger S., *Time Sanctified: The Book of Hours in Medieval Art and Life* (New York, 1988)

— *Painted Prayers: The Book of Hours in Medieval and Renaissance Art* (New York, 1997)

INDEX

References are to pages unless otherwise indicated (pl.= plate).